RESTful Web Services with Dropwizard

Over 20 recipes to help you build high-performance, production-ready RESTful JVM-based backend services

Alexandros Dallas

[PACKT] open source ✿
community experience distilled
PUBLISHING

BIRMINGHAM - MUMBAI

RESTful Web Services with Dropwizard

First published: February 2014

Production Reference: 1120214

Published by Packt Publishing Ltd.
Livery Place
35 Livery Street
Birmingham B3 2PB, UK.

ISBN 978-1-78328-953-0

www.packtpub.com

Cover Image by Jarek Blaminsky (milak6@wp.pl)

Credits

Author
Alexandros Dallas

Reviewers
Sunil Gulabani

Tan Tze Hon

Cemalettin Koc

Acquisition Editor
Vinay Argekar

Content Development Editor
Rikshith Shetty

Technical Editors
Pragnesh Bilimoria

Nikhil Potdukhe

Copy Editors
Mradula Hegde

Gladson Monteiro

Project Coordinator
Sageer Parkar

Proofreader
Paul Hindle

Indexer
Priya Subramani

Production Coordinator
Komal Ramchandani

Cover Work
Komal Ramchandani

About the Author

Alexandros Dallas studied Applied Informatics in Management and Economy and is now a software test engineer based in Athens.

He has a solid programming/software development background, and whenever he is free, he spends his time contributing to open source projects.

He is well aware of Dropwizard's core libraries, such as Jersey, since his interests include the development and integration of web APIs.

About the Reviewers

Sunil Gulabani is a software engineer based in Ahmedabad, Gujarat, India. He graduated with a Bachelor's degree in Commerce from S. M. Patel Institute of Commerce (SMPIC) and a Master's degree in Computer Applications from Ahmedabad Education Society Institute of Computer Studies (AESICS). He has also presented the paper *Effective Label Matching For Automated Evaluation of Use Case Diagrams* at Technology For Education (T4E), IIIT-Hyderabad, an IEEE conference, along with senior lecturer Vinay Vachharajani and Dr. Jyoti Pareek.

He has been working since 2011 as a software engineer and is a cloud technology savvy. He has experience in developing enterprise solutions using Java (EE), Apache SOLR, RESTful Web Services, GWT, SmartGWT, Amazon Web Services (AWS), Redis, Memcache, and MongoDB, among others. He holds a keen interest in system architecture and integration, data modeling, and relational databases and mapping with NoSQL for high throughput.

He is the author of the book *Developing RESTful Web Services with Jersey 2.0* that focuses on the use of JAX-RS 2.0, which is an enhanced framework based on the RESTful architecture.

Apart from that, he takes interest in writing tech blogs and is actively involved in knowledge-sharing communities.

Visit him online at `http://www.sunilgulabani.com`, follow him on Twitter at `twitter.com/sunil_gulabani`, or reach him directly at `sunil_gulabani@yahoo.com`.

I would like to express my heartiest thanks to my parents and family members, who supported me at each and every level of my career, as well as my friends and colleagues, without whom jumping to the next step of my career would not have been possible.

Tan Tze Hon has been fascinated by computers since his youth, and still remembers the days when trying to play a game meant wrestling with `autoexec.bat` files and resolving IRQ conflicts with great fondness. Having felt the pain of hand rolling his own RESTful Web Services, he has embraced Dropwizard to make programming fun again, and has since deployed a variety of Dropwizard services to production. He is currently a polyglot developer at ThoughtWorks, a company that specializes in agile software development. Once in a while, he writes about all things on technology at `tzehon.com`, when he feels that he has spent way too much time on *Hacker News*.

Cemalettin Koc is a software engineer who specializes in designing and creating effective, scalable solutions for web environments. He is very interested in researching on sample applications, and has over eight years of experience in software design, development, and support. He also enjoys doing research related to areas of social network analysis, social computing, recommendation algorithms, data visualization, data mining, information retrieval, business intelligence, and intelligent user interfaces. He has engineered strong, data-driven web applications using a great variety of frameworks. He also works with mobile technologies and has built apps for both iOS and Android OS.

He lives in Istanbul, Turkey, with his wife Ceren and son Mert. Visit him on Twitter at `@CemoKoc` to learn more about him and see what he is currently exploring.

www.PacktPub.com

Support files, eBooks, discount offers and more

You might want to visit www.PacktPub.com for support files and downloads related to your book.

Did you know that Packt offers eBook versions of every book published, with PDF and ePub files available? You can upgrade to the eBook version at www.PacktPub.com and as a print book customer, you are entitled to a discount on the eBook copy. Get in touch with us at service@packtpub.com for more details.

At www.PacktPub.com, you can also read a collection of free technical articles, sign up for a range of free newsletters and receive exclusive discounts and offers on Packt books and eBooks.

http://PacktLib.PacktPub.com

Do you need instant solutions to your IT questions? PacktLib is Packt's online digital book library. Here, you can access, read and search across Packt's entire library of books.

Why Subscribe?

- ► Fully searchable across every book published by Packt
- ► Copy and paste, print and bookmark content
- ► On demand and accessible via web browser

Free Access for Packt account holders

If you have an account with Packt at www.PacktPub.com, you can use this to access PacktLib today and view nine entirely free books. Simply use your login credentials for immediate access.

Table of Contents

Preface

Dropwizard is a Java development framework for RESTful Web Services. It was initially built by Yammer to be used as the base of their backend systems. Dropwizard is production-ready; it encapsulates everything you will need for RESTful development.

Jersey, Jackson, jDBI, and Hibernate are only some of the libraries bundled with Dropwizard. Applications built on Dropwizard run on an embedded Jetty server—you don't need to worry where to deploy your application or whether it is compatible with your target container.

Using Dropwizard, you will be able to build a fast, secure, and scalable web service application efficiently with minimum effort and time.

Dropwizard is open source, and all of its modules are available though Maven repositories. That way, you are able to integrate every library you wish—if it's not already present—just by adding the appropriate dependency entry on your `pom.xml` file. Basic knowledge and understanding of Maven is required.

What this book covers

Chapter 1, *Getting Started with Dropwizard*, will guide you through the basics of Dropwizard, helping you to get familiar with its concepts and also prepare your development environment.

Chapter 2, *Creating a Dropwizard Application*, will introduce Maven and how to use it to create a Dropwizard application. This covers generating the structure of an empty application, based on the default artifact, and the necessary modifications required in order to start building a Dropwizard application.

Chapter 3, *Configuring the Application*, presents the methods available to externalize your application's configuration by enabling the use of a configuration file along with a configuration class that is tasked with fetching, validating, and making the configuration values available throughout the application.

Chapter 4, Creating and Adding REST Resources, will guide you through the implementations of your application's most important aspect: the resource class. You will learn how to map URI paths and HTTP verbs to methods of the resource class and how to add new resources to a Dropwizard application.

Chapter 5, Representations – RESTful Entities, deals with the modeling of representations to actual Java classes and how the POJOs are automatically transformed to JSON representations by Jackson.

Chapter 6, Using a Database, demonstrates the integration and usage of jDBI, how to create data access objects from interfaces, and using jDBI's SQL Object API in order to interact with the database. The additional configuration modifications needed are also presented in this chapter.

Chapter 7, Validating Web Service Requests, presents the usage of Hibernate Validator in order to validate requests from a web service client prior to fulfilling them.

Chapter 8, The Web Service Client, demonstrates how to create a managed Jersey HTTP client to be used by a Dropwizard application in order to interact with web services through `WebResource` objects.

Chapter 9, Authentication, goes through the basics of web service authentication and guides you through the implementation of a basic HTTP authenticator and how to adapt it to the resource class as well as the HTTP client of your application.

Chapter 10, The User Interface – Views, shows the usage of the Dropwizard views bundle and the Mustache template engine in order to create an HTML interface for the web service client.

Appendix A, Testing a Dropwizard Application, demonstrates the usage of Dropwizard's testing module for the creation of automated integration tests. This appendix also deals with the implementation of runtime tests for our application, which are known as health checks. You will be guided through the implementation of a health check that ensures that your HTTP client can indeed interact with a web service.

Appendix B, Deploying a Dropwizard Application, explains the necessary steps you need to take in order to deploy a Dropwizard application to a web server by using a separate configuration file and securing the access to you application's admin port.

What you need for this book

In order to follow the examples and the code snippets presented throughout the book, you will need a computer with a Linux, Windows, or OS X operating system. A modern Java code editor/ IDE such as Eclipse, Netbeans, or IDEA is really going to help you. You will also need Version 7 of Java Development Kit (JDK) as well as Maven and MySQL server. Additional dependencies will be fetched by Maven, so you will need a working Internet connection.

Who this book is for

This book's target audience is software engineers and web developers that have at least basic Java knowledge and a basic understanding of RESTful Web Services. Knowledge of SQL/MySQL usage and command-line scripting may also be needed.

Conventions

In this book, you will find a number of styles of text that distinguish between different kinds of information. Here are some examples of these styles, and an explanation of their meaning.

Code words in text, database table names, folder names, filenames, file extensions, pathnames, dummy URLs, user input, and Twitter handles are shown as follows: "Add a new method in the `Contact` class named `#isValidPerson()`."

A block of code is set as follows:

```
import java.util.Set;
import javax.validation.ConstraintViolation;
import javax.util.ArrayList;
import javax.validation.Validator;
import javax.ws.rs.core.Response.Status;
```

When we wish to draw your attention to a particular part of a code block, the relevant lines or items are set in bold:

```
private final ContactDAO contactDao; private final Validator
    validator;
  public ContactResource(DBI jdbi, Validator validator) {
  contactDao = jdbi.onDemand(ContactDAO.class); this.validator =
    validator;
  }
```

Any command-line input or output is written as follows:

```
$> java -jar target/app.jar server conf.yaml
```

New terms and **important words** are shown in bold. Words that you see on the screen, in menus or dialog boxes for example, appear in the text like this: "At some point, you will be prompted to provide the **MySQL Root Password**."

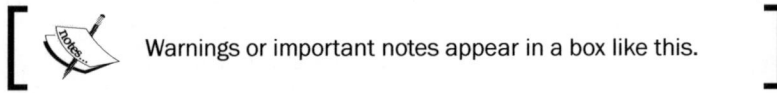

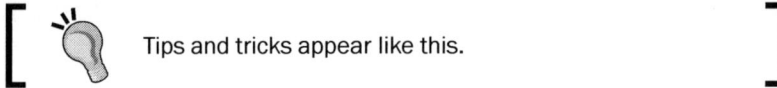

> Warnings or important notes appear in a box like this.

> Tips and tricks appear like this.

Reader feedback

Feedback from our readers is always welcome. Let us know what you think about this book—what you liked or may have disliked. Reader feedback is important for us to develop titles that you really get the most out of.

To send us general feedback, simply send an e-mail to feedback@packtpub.com, and mention the book title via the subject of your message.

If there is a topic that you have expertise in and you are interested in either writing or contributing to a book, see our author guide on www.packtpub.com/authors.

Customer support

Now that you are the proud owner of a Packt book, we have a number of things to help you to get the most from your purchase.

Downloading the example code

You can download the example code files for all Packt books you have purchased from your account at http://www.packtpub.com. If you purchased this book elsewhere, you can visit http://www.packtpub.com/support and register to have the files e-mailed directly to you.

Errata

Although we have taken every care to ensure the accuracy of our content, mistakes do happen. If you find a mistake in one of our books—maybe a mistake in the text or the code—we would be grateful if you would report this to us. By doing so, you can save other readers from frustration and help us improve subsequent versions of this book. If you find any errata, please report them by visiting http://www.packtpub.com/submit-errata, selecting your book, clicking on the **errata submission form** link, and entering the details of your errata. Once your errata are verified, your submission will be accepted and the errata will be uploaded on our website, or added to any list of existing errata, under the Errata section of that title. Any existing errata can be viewed by selecting your title from http://www.packtpub.com/support.

Piracy

Piracy of copyright material on the Internet is an ongoing problem across all media. At Packt, we take the protection of our copyright and licenses very seriously. If you come across any illegal copies of our works, in any form, on the Internet, please provide us with the location address or website name immediately so that we can pursue a remedy.

Please contact us at copyright@packtpub.com with a link to the suspected pirated material.

We appreciate your help in protecting our authors, and our ability to bring you valuable content.

Questions

You can contact us at questions@packtpub.com if you are having a problem with any aspect of the book, and we will do our best to address it.

1
Getting Started with Dropwizard

Dropwizard is an open source Java framework for the rapid development of RESTful Web Services putting together everything you'll need. You can have a production-ready application, making use of **Jetty**, **Jersey**, **Jackson**, **JDBI**, and **Hibernate**, as well as a large number of additional libraries that Dropwizard includes, either in its core or as modules. This solves the problem of manually adding, configuring, and wiring together lots of different libraries while building a web service application from scratch. Think of it like this: you will need Jersey to expose the web services, some other library for database interaction, and additional ones for validation and authentication, not to mention the overhead of dependency management, packaging, and distribution.

Throughout the chapters of this book, we are going to use Dropwizard and its components in order to build a sample application—that is, a phonebook application that exposes a set of RESTful Web Services that facilitate the storing and management of contacts. It works pretty much like your mobile phone's built-in phonebook application or any other contact management application.

Web service development with Dropwizard

We are going to use Jersey in order to build our web services. Jersey is the reference implementation of the **JAX-RS** standard (JSR 311), the Java API for RESTful Web Services. JAX-RS makes use of annotations, simplifying the development of web service applications.

The web services we'll build are going to produce JSON output. Dropwizard includes Jackson, which is a fast, configurable JSON processor, and is used by Jersey to transform plain Java objects to JSON representations.

Our application is going to use a database in order to store data. For our database interaction needs, we'll use JDBI. JDBI is a library that will allow us to easily create DAO interfaces. Data Access Objects would allow us to perform database operations by mapping Java methods to SQL queries and statements. JDBI comes as a Dropwizard module, allowing us to build Data Access Objects easily and fast.

Dropwizard includes validation, monitoring, and testing modules, which we'll use to ensure that our services will behave correctly in production environments. We are going to integrate Dropwizard's validation mechanisms, ensuring that each and every request to our web services is valid, before trying to serve it.

Preparing your development environment

Before we start creating Dropwizard applications, we need to set up our development environment, which will consist of, at least, **Java (JDK 7)**, **Maven**, and **MySQL**.

Getting ready

Maven is a build manager for Java projects. We will use it to create and build our project. Our application's dependencies (on Dropwizard's modules) will be managed by Maven; we just need to add the appropriate entries in our project configuration file.

We need a database, so we will use MySQL for the needs of this book. MySQL is the most popular open source relational database management system—a common choice for web applications. Throughout the installation process, you will be prompted to create or configure the values of environment variables. This procedure varies from one operating system to another, and is something out of the scope of this book.

How to do it...

We will take a look at all the components that you will need to download and install.

Downloading and installing Java

1. Download Java 7 JDK from `http://www.oracle.com/technetwork/java/javase/downloads/jdk7-downloads-1880260.html`.

2. Since many installation packages are available, you need to select the appropriate one, depending on your operating system and platform.

3. After the download has completed, install the JDK by running the installer you downloaded, as shown in the following screenshot. There's no need to use settings different than the default ones for now. After a few steps, the installation will be completed.

Chapter 1

4. Following the successful installation, set the JAVA_HOME environment variable with its value set to the path where you installed Java. In Windows, this may be something like C:\Program Files\Java\jdk1.7.0_40\.

Downloading and installing Maven

1. Maven installation is pretty straightforward. Just download Maven binaries from http://maven.apache.org/download.cgi and extract the contents of the package in a directory of your choice.

2. Modify the PATH environment variable, adding the Maven directory suffixed with \bin, like C:\apache-maven-3.0.5\bin, so the mvn executable will be available on all directories when using the command line or the terminal.

Downloading and installing MySQL

1. Download the **MySQL Community Server** installer for your operating system from http://dev.mysql.com/downloads/mysql/#downloads.

2. Run the installer and select to install MySQL. Keep the proposed, default installation settings.

3. At some point, you will be prompted to provide the **MySQL Root Password**. This is the password of the root user, which has full access rights. Enter a password of your choice, and proceed by clicking on the **Next >** button. The installation will be completed shortly.

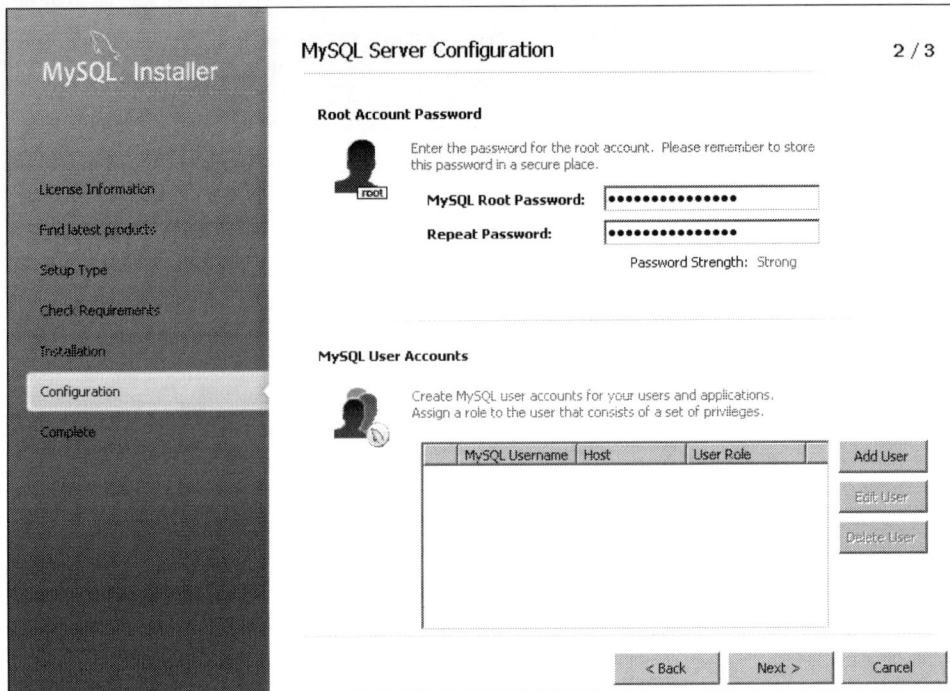

4. Please choose a password that you will remember easily, as you will need to provide it at a later stage.

How it works...

We just completed the installation of the software packages required to build Dropwizard applications. We will use Maven to create the structure of our application, which will use MySQL as a persistent store for its data.

We are going to create a Maven project, and in its **Project Object Model** (POM) file, we will include the references (dependencies) to the Dropwizard components our application will use. Maven will automatically download and make them available for use throughout our project.

2
Creating a Dropwizard Application

Let's go through the processes required to create a new RESTful Web Services application based on Dropwizard. Firstly, we will need to create the application's structure, files, and folders, and also obtain the necessary libraries. Luckily, Maven will handle these tasks for us.

As soon as our application's structure is ready, we will modify the appropriate files, defining the application's dependencies on Dropwizard's modules and also configuring how the runnable package of our application should be produced. After that, we may proceed to coding our application.

Generating a Maven-based project

Before we start with coding, we need to perform some tasks in order to properly create our project's structure. We are going to use Maven in order to generate a default, empty project, which we will then turn into a Dropwizard application.

Getting ready

Our project will be based on the `maven-archetype-quickstart` archetype. Archetypes are Maven project templates, and by using the `quick-start` archetype, we will have our project's structure (folders and files) prepared in no time.

How to do it...

1. Open the terminal (the command line in Windows) and navigate to the directory where you want your application to be created.

2. Create a new Maven project by executing the following command (without the line breaks):

```
$ mvn archetype:generate
    -DgroupId=com.dwbook.phonebook
    -DartifactId=dwbook-phonebook
    -DarchetypeArtifactId=maven-archetype-quickstart
    -DinteractiveMode=false
```

This will create an empty Maven project in the `dwbook-phonebook` directory.

> **Downloading the example code**
>
> You can download the example code files for all Packt books you have purchased from your account at `http://www.packtpub.com`. If you purchased this book elsewhere, you can visit `http://www.packtpub.com/support` and register to have the files e-mailed directly to you.

How it works...

Dropwizard is based on Maven, so we created a new Maven project in which we included Dropwizard's core dependency.

The structure of the `dwbook-phonebook` directory at this point is illustrated in the following screenshot:

The `src/` folder will hold our application's main classes, whereas all the test classes will be placed under the `test/` directory.

Notice that Maven has placed `pom.xml` on the application's root folder. The **Project Object Model** (**POM**) is an XML file that holds important information regarding our project's configuration and dependencies. This is the file we need to edit in order to add Dropwizard support for our project.

Configuring Dropwizard dependencies and building the configuration

We just created a sample application outline. The next thing we need to do is edit the project's configuration file, `pom.xml`, and define the Maven modules on which our application will depend on. We are building a Dropwizard application, and Dropwizard is based on Maven, so everything we need is available in the Maven Central Repository. This means that we just need to provide the modules' IDs, and Maven will take care of the download and inclusion of these modules in our project.

Next, we need to add build and package support to our project. We will use the `maven-shade` plugin, which will allow us to package our project completely, along with its dependencies, into a single standalone JAR file (Fat JAR) that can be distributed and executed as is.

How to do it...

Perform the following steps to configure Dropwizard dependencies and build the configuration:

1. We need to configure our POM by adding the Maven Repository where snapshots of all Dropwizard modules can be found. Maven will then be able to automatically fetch the required modules during the building of our project. Locate the `<dependencies>` section in `pom.xml` and add the following entries just before it:

   ```
   <repositories>
           <repository>
               <id>sonatype-nexus-snapshots</id>
               <name>Sonatype Nexus Snapshots</name>
               <url>http://oss.sonatype.org/content/repositories/
       snapshots</url>
           </repository>
       </repositories>
   ```

2. To define the dependencies, add the following code within the `<dependencies>` section:

   ```
   <dependency>
       <groupId>io.dropwizard</groupId>
       <artifactId>dropwizard-core</artifactId>
       <version>0.7.0-SNAPSHOT</version>
   </dependency>
   ```

3. To configure the build and package procedures, locate the `<project>` section in `pom.xml` and insert the following entries within it:

```xml
<build>
  <plugins>
    <plugin>
      <groupId>org.apache.maven.plugins</groupId>
      <artifactId>maven-compiler-plugin</artifactId>
      <version>3.1</version>
      <configuration>
        <source>1.7</source>
        <target>1.7</target>
        <encoding>UTF-8</encoding>
      </configuration>
    </plugin>
    <plugin>
      <groupId>org.apache.maven.plugins</groupId>
      <artifactId>maven-shade-plugin</artifactId>
      <version>1.6</version>
      <configuration>
        <filters>
          <filter>
            <artifact>*:*</artifact>
            <excludes>
              <exclude>META-INF/*.SF</exclude>
              <exclude>META-INF/*.DSA</exclude>
              <exclude>META-INF/*.RSA</exclude>
            </excludes>
          </filter>
        </filters>
      </configuration>
      <executions>
        <execution>
          <phase>package</phase>
          <goals>
            <goal>shade</goal>
          </goals>
          <configuration>
            <transformers>
              <transformer
                implementation="org.apache.maven.plugins.
                shade.resource.
                ManifestResourceTransformer">
```

```
              <mainClass>com.dwbook.phonebook.App</mainClass>
                  </transformer>
                </transformers>
              </configuration>
            </execution>
          </executions>
        </plugin>
      </plugins>
    </build>
```

How it works...

We just told Maven everything it needs to know in order to build our application. Maven will fetch the Dropwizard core module from the Maven Central Repository and include it in the build path while packaging (as a result of the `mvn` package command) the application.

Moreover, we added build and package support with the `maven-shade` plugin and also specified our application's main class (the `<mainClass>` section in `pom.xml`), which facilitates the packaging of the Dropwizard application with its dependencies into a single JAR file. We also instructed the `maven-compiler-plugin` to build the application for Java Version 1.7 (check the target and source elements of the configuration section of `maven-compiler plugin`).

The exclusion of digital signatures

The `<excludes>` section in the `maven-shade` configuration instructs Maven to exclude the digital signatures of all the referenced signed JAR files. This is because Java would otherwise treat them as invalid during runtime, preventing the execution of our application.

Hello World using Dropwizard

Our project's dependencies are now set in the `pom.xml` file and we may start building our application. Maven has already created our application's entry point class, the `App` class, in the `App.java` file. However, its default contents are more suitable to a plain Java application and not a Dropwizard-based one.

How to do it...

Let's have a look at the steps we need to follow to print a `Hello World` message using Dropwizard:

1. In the `App.java` file, add the following import clauses:

    ```
    import org.slf4j.Logger;
    import org.slf4j.LoggerFactory;
    ```

```
import io.dropwizard.Application;
import io.dropwizard.Configuration;
import io.dropwizard.setup.Bootstrap;
import io.dropwizard.setup.Environment;
```

2. Modify the definition of the App class as shown in the next step. This class needs to extend Application <Configuration>.

3. Add a logger to our application by declaring it as a static final member of the App class after its definition:

```
public class App extends Application<Configuration> {
  private static final Logger LOGGER =
    LoggerFactory.getLogger(App.class);
```

4. Implement the abstract methods of the Service class, initialize() and run(), by adding the following code:

```
@Override
public void initialize(Bootstrap<Configuration> b) {}
@Override
public void run(Configuration c, Environment e) throws
  Exception {
  LOGGER.info("Method App#run() called");
  System.out.println( "Hello world, by Dropwizard!" );
}
```

5. Finally, modify the main() method, adding the necessary code to instantiate our Dropwizard service:

```
public static void main( String[] args ) throws Exception
{
    new App().run(args);
  }
```

6. Build the application by executing the following command in your terminal inside the dwbook-phonebook directory:

```
$ mvn package
```

The output of this command will contain the [INFO] BUILD SUCCESS line, indicating that the project was successfully built, as shown in the following screenshot:

```
[INFO] ------------------------------------------------------------------------
[INFO] BUILD SUCCESS
[INFO] ------------------------------------------------------------------------
[INFO] Total time: 6.622s
[INFO] Finished at: Sun Sep 22 14:54:45 EEST 2013
[INFO] Final Memory: 37M/171M
[INFO] ------------------------------------------------------------------------
$
```

Maven has produced (built) the executable Fat JAR using the shade plugin, and this can be located in the target/directory named `dwbook-phonebook-1.0-SNAPSHOT.jar`. Run it as you would with any executable JAR file using the `java -jar` command as follows:

```
$ java -jar target/dwbook-phonebook-1.0-SNAPSHOT.jar server
```

Normally, you should see a lot of entries in your terminal, including an error. The first line is the message in which we included the `#run()` method. This is followed by a warning message indicating that our application has no health checks configured, but this is something we will handle later on in this book.

The next logged entries indicate that the Jetty server embedded in our Dropwizard application is starting and listening for incoming requests on port 8080. Port 8081 is also used for administration purposes. You will also see an error stating that no resource classes could be located (the `ResourceConfig` instance does not contain any root resource classes), which is reasonable and absolutely normal, as we haven't created and configured any REST resources yet.

How it works...

What we just did was we added the minimum amount of code required in a Dropwizard application. As you saw, our application's entry point class needs to extend the `io.dropwizard.Application` class and implement the `initialize(Bootstrap<Configuration>)` and `run(Configuration, Environment)` methods. The `initialize` method is tasked with bootstrapping, possibly loading additional components and generally preparing the runtime environment of the application.

We were going to just print a `Hello` message in this phase, so we included only a `println()` statement in the `run()` method.

The execution of the JAR file produced by the `mvn` package command resulted in the printing of the **Hello World!** greeting by Dropwizard, as `public static void main` triggered the execution of the relevant code in the `public void run` method.

There's more...

For executing the JAR file, we add the `server` argument to the command. In `public static void main`, we called the `public void run` method, passing command-line arguments to it. Dropwizard has only one command preconfigured (although we're able to configure additional commands), the `server` command, which starts the embedded HTTP Server (Jetty) to run our service. In our case, following the execution of the code in the `run()` method, an error with an exception was displayed as Jetty couldn't locate any REST resources to serve.

Logging

Dropwizard is backed by Logback and provides an SLF4J implementation for our logging means. In the `App.java` file, we imported the necessary `Logger` and `LoggerFactory` classes in order to construct a `Logger` instance we could use for our logging needs.

Default HTTP Ports

Dropwizard's embedded Jetty server will try to bind to ports 8080 and 8081 by default. Port 8080 is used by the server in order to serve incoming HTTP requests to the application, while 8081 is used by Dropwizard's administration interface. In case there is another service running on your system that uses any of these ports, you will see a `java.net.BindException` when trying to run this example.

Later on, we will see how you can configure your application to use another port for incoming requests, but for now, just make sure this port is available to use.

3
Configuring the Application

Up until this point, we have created a simple template for a Dropwizard application. What our application does is print a message to the terminal during startup.

Generally, every modern application depends on a number of configuration settings that define the way it runs. For instance, once our application grows and needs to interact with a database, we should somehow use (at least) a username and password to establish a database connection. Of course, we can hardcode these settings inside the application, but that's not efficient, as even a small change would require rebuilding it. The appropriate way of storing such or similar information is by using an external configuration file.

Externalizing the application's configuration

Using a configuration file requires the appropriate application logic to load and parse it. Luckily, Dropwizard has built-in functionality that we will use in order to externalize our application's configuration.

How to do it...

1. Create a new YAML file named `config.yaml` in the same directory as the `pom.xml` file. This will be the configuration file of our application. We will add two configuration parameters: the message to be printed on startup and how many times to print it. In order to do so, add the following code to `config.yaml`:

```
message: This is a message defined in the configuration
  file config.yaml.
messageRepetitions: 3
```

2. Now we have a configuration file, but we need to parse it. Let's create a new class in the `com.dwbook.phonebook` package named `PhonebookConfiguration` by adding the following code:

```
package com.dwbook.phonebook;

import com.fasterxml.jackson.annotation.JsonProperty;
import io.dropwizard.Configuration;

public class PhonebookConfiguration extends Configuration {
  @JsonProperty
  private String message;

  @JsonProperty
  private int messageRepetitions;

  public String getMessage() {
    return message;
  }

  public int getMessageRepetitions() {
    return messageRepetitions;
  }
}
```

> As you can see, it is a simple class, with two member properties named after our configuration settings along with their getter methods.

3. To use this class as our configuration proxy, modify the declaration of our main `App` class to extend the `Application<PhonebookConfiguration>` class instead of `Application<Configuration>`:

```
public class App extends
  Application<PhonebookConfiguration> {
```

4. Similarly, update `configuration` to `PhonebookConfiguration` in the declaration of the `App#initialize()` method:

```
@Override

public void initialize(Bootstrap<PhonebookConfiguration> b)
  {}
```

5. The `App#run()` method will require the same modification in its definition, but we'll also modify this method further so it retrieves the message to print from the configuration class:

```
public void run(PhonebookConfiguration c, Environment e)
    throws Exception {
  LOGGER.info("Method App#run() called");
  for (int i=0; i < c.getMessageRepetitions(); i++) {
    System.out.println(c.getMessage());
  }
}
```

6. Package (`mvn package`) and run the application and specify the configuration file as well:

```
$ java -jar target/dwbook-phonebook-1.0-SNAPSHOT.jar server
  config.yaml
```

You will see the message printed three times in your terminal during the application's startup, as shown in the following screenshot:

```
$ java -jar target/dwbook-phonebook-1.0-SNAPSHOT.jar server config.yaml
INFO  [2013-09-26 15:22:15,744] com.dwbook.phonebook.App: Method App#run() called
This is a message defined in the configuration file config.yaml.
This is a message defined in the configuration file config.yaml.
This is a message defined in the configuration file config.yaml.
WARN  [2013-09-26 15:22:15 763] com.yammer.dropwizard.config.ServerFactory:
```

Apart from this, and as in the previous example, you will also see an exception stating that no resource classes could be located (the `ResourceConfig` instance does not contain any root resource classes). This is because we do not have any REST resources registered in our application yet. We will deal with this in the following chapter.

How it works...

You should see that our configuration file is automatically parsed. In fact, the `PhonebookConfiguration` class is instantiated with the values specified in the configuration file.

When a configuration file is passed as a command-line argument, Dropwizard parses it and creates an instance of your service's configuration class. We added the required configuration parameters as private members of the `PhonebookConfiguration` class and annotated them with `@JsonProperty` so Dropwizard can parse them. In order to make these properties accessible to our application's service class, we also need to add public getters for these parameters.

There's more...

Externalizing your application's configuration has many advantages. With Dropwizard, you can easily store and read any kind of properties (configuration settings) you wish to have for your application with minimum effort, just by mapping YAML properties to the properties of your configuration class.

Dropwizard's configuration parameters

Dropwizard has plenty of configuration parameters available, such as the port that the embedded Jetty listens to and the logging level. The list is quite large and cannot be covered here extensively, though it is available on the official Dropwizard website at `http://www.dropwizard.io/manual/core/#configuration-defaults`.

YAML

The description of YAML according to its official website (`http://www.yaml.org`) is human-friendly data serialization standard. Its syntax is pretty straightforward, which is also the reason why YAML is widely accepted. YAML files are identified by the extensions `.yaml` and `.yml`; both are valid, although `.yml` seems to be more popular lately.

Validating configuration settings

Although it is good to have the application's configuration externalized, we should not always rely on it as is. Dropwizard has got us covered, and we have the right tools in order to validate the configuration properties up on the application's startup. This is because we can use constraint annotations for our configuration properties, such as those included in the `javax.validation.constraints` or `org.hibernate.validator.constraints` packages.

We are going to limit the number of repetitions of the message to 10; if the number provided is larger than 10, then the input is considered invalid.

How to do it...

Let's go through the following steps required for validating the configuration settings:

1. Update the definition of the `messageRepetitions` property in `PhonebookConfiguration`, annotating the property with the `@Max` annotation (you will also need to import `javax.validation.constraints.Max`):

```
@JsonProperty
@Max(10)
private int messageRepetitions;
```

2. In a similar way, define that the `message` property should not be empty, annotating the property with the `@NotEmpty` (`org.hibernate.validator.constraints.NotEmpty`) annotation:

```
@JsonProperty
@NotEmpty
private String message;
```

3. Edit the `Config.yaml` file and specify a value greater than 10 for the `messageRepetitions` property.

4. Repackage and run the application again. The application will refuse to start, and you will see an error printed on your terminal as seen in the following screenshot:

```
Terminal
$ java -jar target/dwbook-phonebook-1.0.0-SNAPSHOT.jar server config.yaml
config.yaml has an error:
  * messageRepetitions must be less than or equal to 10 (was 23)

$ 
```

How it works...

The validation-related annotations force Dropwizard to validate the values of each of the properties declared in our configuration file. If the validation constraints are not satisfied, the relevant error message will be printed on the terminal, and the application will not start.

There's more...

Now you have a working configuration file that is mapped on the configuration object during the startup of the application. Also, as well as checking the validity of the configuration parameters, you can also provide a default value for each one of them.

Specifying default parameters

You can specify the default values for configuration parameters as easily as initializing the variables on their declaration. This way, optional parameters can be omitted and can have a default value during runtime, even if they're not included in the application's configuration file.

Let's add an additional parameter, which we'll also initialize, named `additionalMessage`, along with its getter method:

```
@JsonProperty
private String additionalMessage = "This is optional";
public String getAdditionalMessage() {
   return additionalMessage;
}
```

If you run the application specifying a configuration file that does not contain the `additionalMessage` property, then the default value of this property will be returned when you try to access it from another part of the code, for instance, if you use `c.getAdditionalMessage()` from inside the `App#run()` method. This way, you can have optional parameters for your application.

Creating and Adding REST Resources

Up until this point, our application doesn't really do much. This is because it lacks configured REST resources. A REST resource is something that one can refer to as an entity, and in our case, a set of URI templates with a common base URL that one can interact with using common HTTP methods.

Creating a resource class

We are building a phonebook application, and thus we need to implement the necessary functionalities for storing and managing contacts. We will create the resource class for the phonebook service. This class will be responsible for handling HTTP requests and generating JSON responses. The resource class will initially provide the endpoints for retrieving, creating, updating, and deleting contacts.

Please note that we are not yet dealing with structured data or interacting with a database, and thus contact-related information transmitted to and from our application does not follow a specific format.

How to do it...

Perform the following steps for creating a resource class:

1. Create a new package, `com.dwbook.phonebook.resources`, and add a `ContactResource` class in it.

2. Import the required packages, `javax.ws.rs.*` and `javax.ws.rs.core.*.wdasdasd`:

```
import javax.ws.rs.*;
import javax.ws.rs.core.*;
```

3. Specify the URI template of the resource by annotating the class with the `@Path` annotation and also specify the response `Content-Type` header using the `@Produces` annotation:

```
@Path("/contact")
@Produces(MediaType.APPLICATION_JSON)
public class ContactResource {
   // code...
}
```

4. In order to add a method that will return the information regarding a stored contact, create the `#getContact()` method. This method will return a `javax.ws.rs.core.Response` object, which is a simple but efficient way of manipulating the actual HTTP response sent to the client that performs the request. Add the `@GET` and `@PATH` annotations as shown in the following code snippet. This will bind the method to HTTP GET requests to `/contact/{id}`. The `{id}` part of the URI represents a variable, and is bound to the `int id` parameter of the same method via the `@PathParam` annotation:

```
@GET
@Path("/{id}")
public Response getContact(@PathParam("id") int id) {
   // retrieve information about the contact with the
provided id
   // ...
   return Response
       .ok("{contact_id: " + id + ", name: \"Dummy Name\",
phone: \"+0123456789\" }")
       .build();
}
```

5. Similarly, we need to implement appropriate methods for creating, deleting, and updating contacts. The `#createContact()` method for creating contacts will be bound to HTTP POST requests to the `/contact` URI. Since nothing is appended to our base URI, this method does not need to be annotated with `@Path`. This method will return a `Response` object as well, like all of our resource's methods will, indicating that a new contact has been created:

```
@POST
public Response createContact(
    @FormParam("name") String name,
```

```
      @FormParam("phone") String phone) {
  // store the new contact
  // ...
  return Response
      .created(null)
      .build();
}
```

6. For deleting existing contacts, the HTTP client needs to send an HTTP DELETE request to a particular contact's URI. Due to this, the respective method's URI will be exactly the same as the one for retrieving a single contact. Add the `#deleteContact()` method to our resource class, as shown in the following code snippet. We will also need to indicate that the requested URI does not have content anymore:

```
@DELETE
@Path("/{id}")
public Response deleteContact(@PathParam("id") int id) {
  // delete the contact with the provided id
  // ...
  return Response
      .noContent()
      .build();
}
```

7. The updates to existing contacts are generally performed by HTTP PUT requests to a contact's endpoint. The `#updateContact()` method is going to handle such requests and indicate that the update was successful, returning the appropriate `Response` object:

```
@PUT
@Path("/{id}")
public Response updateContact(
    @PathParam("id") int id,
    @FormParam("name") String name,
    @FormParam("phone") String phone) {
  // update the contact with the provided ID
  // ...
  return Response
      .ok("{contact_id: "+ id +", name: \""+ name +"\",
phone: \""+ phone +"\" }")
      .build();
}
```

8. Add the implemented resource to our Dropwizard application's environment by modifying the `run` method in the `App` class via the `JerseyEnvironment#register()` method, as shown in the following code. You also need to add an import clause on top of the `App.java` file for the `ContactResource` class (import `com.dwbook.phonebook.resources.ContactResource`). You should also see that in order to access our application's Jersey environment, you may use the `Environment#jersey()` method:

```
public void run(PhonebookConfiguration c, Environment e)
    throws Exception {
  // ...
  // Add the resource to the environment
  e.jersey().register(new ContactResource());
}
```

9. Rebuild (with `mvn package`) and run the application `java -jar target/dwbook-phonebook-1.0-SNAPSHOT.jar server config.yaml`. You will see a message indicating that our (Jersey based) Dropwizard application is starting along with a list of configured resources, in this case, the resources defined in our `com.dwbook.phonebook.resources.ContactResource` class.

```
Terminal
INFO  [2013-10-02 19:23:32,202] com.yammer.dropwizard.cli.ServerCommand: Starting App
INFO  [2013-10-02 19:23:32,204] org.eclipse.jetty.server.Server: jetty-8.y.z-SNAPSHOT
INFO  [2013-10-02 19:23:32,319] com.sun.jersey.server.impl.application.WebApplicationImpl: Initiating Jersey application, ve
rsion 'Jersey: 1.17.1 02/28/2013 12:47 PM'
INFO  [2013-10-02 19:23:32,419] com.yammer.dropwizard.config.Environment: The following paths were found for the configured
resources:

    DELETE   /contact/{id} (com.dwbook.phonebook.resources.ContactResource)
    GET      /contact/{id} (com.dwbook.phonebook.resources.ContactResource)
    POST     /contact (com.dwbook.phonebook.resources.ContactResource)
    PUT      /contact/{id} (com.dwbook.phonebook.resources.ContactResource)

INFO  [2013-10-02 19:23:32,419] com.yammer.dropwizard.config.Environment: tasks =

    POST     /tasks/gc (com.yammer.dropwizard.tasks.GarbageCollectionTask)

INFO  [2013-10-02 19:23:32,787] org.eclipse.jetty.server.AbstractConnector: Started InstrumentedBlockingChannelConnector@0.0
.0.0:8080
INFO  [2013-10-02 19:23:32,791] org.eclipse.jetty.server.AbstractConnector: Started SocketConnector@0.0.0.0:8081
```

10. Point your browser at `http://localhost:8080/contact/100` and see the results; it will generate a dummy JSON representation with the ID 100, which you provided in the URL (a path parameter, which will work with any integer).

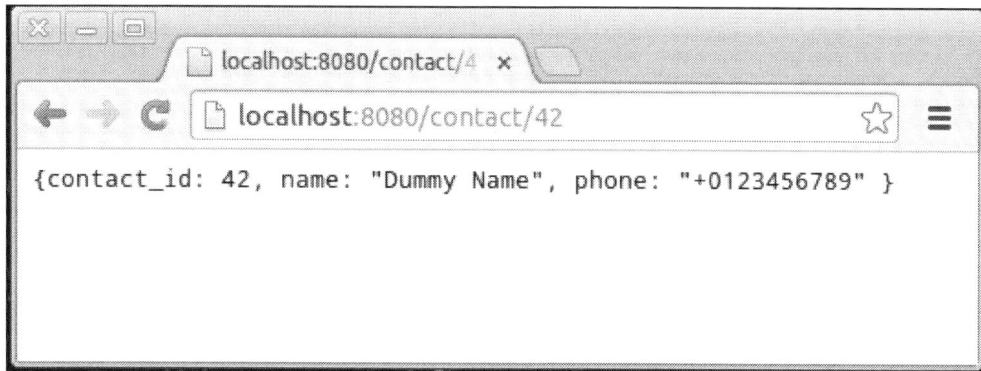

```
{contact_id: 42, name: "Dummy Name", phone: "+0123456789" }
```

The service is running and listening to incoming requests. You can shut it down by pressing *Ctrl + C* in your terminal. After a few seconds, the service will stop.

How it works...

The resource class is the most important part of a RESTful Web Service, as it is the place where you define the resources and their URIs you wish to expose.

The @Produces annotation defines the content type of the responses the class methods generate. Despite of defining the value of the HTTP Content-Type header, it is also used to instruct Jackson to transform the representations to the appropriate format, JSON in this case; thus the MediaType.APPLICATION_JSON definition. In case we would want to return an XML document as the response, we should use MediaType.APPLICATION_XML instead.

We use the @Path annotation to define a URI template. By applying it and bringing it on to the level of a class, we define that the base URI of our resources will be /contact. We used this annotation for the #getContact method as well, specifying the/{id} template. This leads on to the complete URI that will trigger the execution of #getContact being /contact/{id}.

The {id} part of the URI is a path parameter, which we mapped to the int id argument using the @PathParam annotation. PathParam takes the name of the path parameter as its parameter, which in this case is id.

Jersey will intercept every incoming HTTP request and try to match it with the defined URI template in order to find which resource class method to invoke.

It is generally a good practice to define the base URI at the class level, and additionally, more specific URI templates per method.

In order to configure our application to use the resources we created, we had to add them to the execution environment, post initialization, in the #run() method of the App class.

There's more...

A representation is an entity; something that one can refer to. A representation can be created, updated, deleted, and returned. A REST resource is an endpoint that accepts HTTP requests for such operations.

We used the @GET annotation for the #getContact() method. This implies that the method is bound to, and only to, the HTTP GET verb. We used this verb because we were returning data about an entity without modifying it in any way.

HTTP verbs – RESTful convention

Generally, a RESTful Web Service uses four fundamental HTTP methods (verbs) mapped to CRUD operations:

- POST for creating a resource
- PUT for updating a resource
- DELETE for deleting a resource
- GET for returning the representation of a resource

GET is an idempotent operation; if given the same input, it will return the same results without modifying the requesting entity in any case.

> You can map HTTP verbs to a resource method (for example, #getContact()) using an appropriate annotation (such as @POST, @PUT, @DELETE, and @GET).

HTTP response codes

Another important RESTful Web Service design principle, apart from CRUD operations being mapped to specific HTTP methods, is the usage of specific response codes according to the request and the outcome of the action it triggered.

According to this convention, when a new entity is created successfully, our application would respond indicating 201 Created as the HTTP Response Status code.

Similarly, when an entity is successfully deleted, our application would send the 204 No Content code. The 204 No Content code may also be used in other cases where the response we send to the client does not include an entity, and not only in cases where we delete resources.

For most cases though, when our application is returning data while responding to GET requests, the 200 OK response code is sufficient.

We used the response class in our implementation in order to include specific response codes to our application's responses.

The Response class

The javax.ws.rs.Response class, instances of which all of our methods return, provides a set of ResponseBuilder methods that we can use for constructing the data we return to the client that performs the HTTP request to our service.

The method Response#ok() accepts an Object instance as the parameter, which is then serialized to our service's response format (defined by the @Produces annotation) accordingly. The usage of this method returns an HTTP 200 OK response code to the client.

The Response#noContent() method returns an HTTP 204 No Content response code to the client, indicating that no content is applicable to this request.

On the other hand, the Response#created() method is used to send a 201 Created response code along with the URI of the newly created resource. The URI (or null) can be passed as a parameter to this method and will be used as the value for the Location header of the response.

The Response class has a number of useful methods like these, but it also enables us to set custom response codes without necessarily using one of the predefined methods. To do so, you can use the Response#status() method by providing it with the appropriate response code, as shown in the following example:

```
Response.status(Status.MOVED_PERMANENTLY);
```

Additionally, we are able to use the ResponseBuilder#entity() method in order to set the appropriate response payload. The #entity() method accepts Object as the parameter and processes it in a way similar to the Response#created() method:

```
Response.status(Status.MOVED_PERMANENTLY).entity(new Object());
```

What should be noted is that all these methods return a ResponseBuilder instance and can be chained as well. In order to build the Response object, we must use the ResponseBuilder#build() method.

5
Representations – RESTful Entities

Our web service is now responding to requests that produce output by utilizing the `Response` class. We saw that there are methods of this class that take an object as a parameter.

Creating a representation class

We are going to create the representations that will be produced by the REST resources of our application. A simple Java class is everything needed by Jersey, so it will consider the class as a RESTful representation.

Given that our web service needs to produce contact-related information in the JSON format, a sample response would look something like the following code:

```
{ id: 1, firstName: "John", lastName: "Doe", phone: "+123-456-789" }
```

We will build our representation class around this JSON string. The class will have the necessary properties (`id`, `firstName`, `lastName`, and `phone`) along with their getter methods.

How to do it...

Perform the following steps for creating a representation class:

1. Create a new package called `com.dwbook.phonebook.representations` and create a `Contact` class in it.

2. Add the aforementioned contact properties as final members, also implementing their getters and a constructor:

```java
package com.dwbook.phonebook.representations;

public class Contact {
  private final int id;
  private final String firstName;
  private final String lastName;
  private final String phone;

  public Contact() {
    this.id = 0;
    this.firstName = null;
    this.lastName = null;
    this.phone = null;
  }

  public Contact(int id, String firstName, String lastName,
  String phone) {
    this.id = id;
    this.firstName = firstName;
    this.lastName = lastName;
    this.phone = phone;
  }

  public int getId() {
    return id;
  }
  public String getFirstName() {
    return firstName;
  }
  public String getLastName() {
    return lastName;
  }
  public String getPhone() {
    return phone;
  }
}
```

How it works...

The representation class for contacts is now ready. All that was required was just a plain Java class with the same properties as the JSON object that we wish our application to generate. In order for this to work though, the appropriate public getter methods are needed.

Our properties were declared final in order to be immutable, and for this reason, we also created a constructor that initializes the properties accordingly.

Instances of this class may now be used in our Jersey-based REST resources as the output. Jackson will handle the transformation from POJO to JSON transparently.

There's more...

Any POJO can be used as a representation. Jackson constructs the JSON string recursively according to the getter methods of each class and their return type.

The Jackson Java JSON processor

Jackson is a powerful open source JSON data binder/parser and processor that facilitates the transformation of plain old Java objects to the JSON format and vice versa. Jersey uses Jackson for its transformation needs and is part of the `dropwizard-core` module; so, it is already included in our project setup.

JSON arrays

Any instance of the `java.util.List` type will be converted to a JSON array. For example, if we wanted to store multiple phone numbers for a contact, we would have declared `private final List<String> phoneNumbers` in the representation class (with the appropriate modifications to the class constructor and the getter).

This would lead to JSON representations of the following format:

```
{ id: 1, firstName: "John", lastName: "Doe", phoneNumbers:
  ["+123-456-789", "+234-567-890", "+345-678-901"] }
```

Ignoring properties

You can prevent a property from being a part of the JSON representation by adding the `@JsonIgnore` annotation to its getter.

This will cause Jackson to ignore a getter method that otherwise would be treated as a JSON property.

Serving representations through the Resource class

Consider the `ContactResource#getContact()` method we previously implemented. We use the `Response#ok(Object entity)` method in order to build the response to be sent to the client, passing it to `String` as a parameter, as shown in the following code:

```
return Response.ok("{id: " + id + ", name: \"Dummy Name\", phone:
    \"+0123456789\" }").build();
```

Now, we have our `Representation` class ready, and we are going to utilize it and pass instances of it to the `#ok()` method.

How to do it...

Perform the following steps to learn the serving of representation through the resource class:

1. Update the `ContactResource#getContact()` method accordingly in order to pass a `Contact` object in the `#ok()` method instead of `String`, as shown in the following code. You will need to import the `Contact` class first (`import com.dwbook.phonebook.representations.Contact`):

```
@GET
@Path("/{id}")
public Response getContact(@PathParam("id") int id) {
  // retrieve information about the contact with the provided id
  // ...
    return Response
    .ok( new Contact( id, "John", "Doe", "+123456789") )
    .build();
}
```

2. Next, modify the method's signature, splitting the `name` variable to `firstName` and `lastName` in order to be consistent with the `Contact` class:

```
@PUT
@Path("/{id}")
public Response updateContact(
    @PathParam("id") int id,
    @FormParam("firstName") String firstName,
    @FormParam("lastName") String lastName,
```

```
        @FormParam("phone") String phone) {
    // update the contact with the provided ID
    // ...
    return Response
        .ok( new Contact(id, firstName, lastName, phone) )
        .build();
}
```

3. Rebuild (`mvn package`) and run the application again:

   ```
   $ java -jar target/dwbook-phonebook-1.0-SNAPSHOT.
     jar server config.yaml
   ```

4. Navigate to `http://localhost:8080/contact/123` or perform a PUT request to the same URL. You will see that the response that the server is sending to our request is a JSON representation of the object we are passing to the `Response#ok()` method.

How it works...

We define the response sent to the client by using the `Response#ok()` method, which accepts an object as a parameter. Until now, we have been passing JSON strings directly. This is not an efficient way, as our application will be handling actual objects (the `Contact` instances), and there is no reason for manually creating JSON representations of them when this can be done automatically by Jackson.

There's more...

We are now using our `representation` class in order to map its properties to the response we are producing. We can also use the same class to map our input parameters. For instance, we could modify the `ContactResource#updateContact()` and `ContactResource#createContact()` methods to expect a `Contact` object as a parameter instead of using each of its properties explicitly.

Using cURL to perform HTTP requests

Using your browser, you can only perform GET requests. In order to effectively test our application though, we will need a tool capable of performing HTTP requests with the POST, PUT, and DELETE methods. cURL (`http://curl.haxx.se/`) is a command-line tool that we can use to better comprehend the examples. You can download it from `http://curl.haxx.se/download.html` by choosing the package that is compatible with your platform.

Performing a GET request is as simple as the cURL. The following example will call the `#getContact()` method:

```
$ curl  http://localhost:8080/contact/123
```

```
⊗ − ⊡   Terminal
$ curl http://localhost:8080/contact/123
{"id":123,"firstName":"John","lastName":"Doe","phone":"+123456789"}

$ ▮
```

The JSON string you are seeing in the second line is the server's response.

In order to perform a PUT request to update a contact, we will need to use the `-X` flag followed by the method name (that is `curl  -X  PUT` ...). To send data to the server along with our request, a contact's information in this case, use the `-d` flag as well along with the data. Note that since the `#updateContact()` method's parameters are mapped to request parameters (with `@FormParam`), we need to send the data URL encoded. Take a look at the following screenshot:

```
⊗ − ⊡   Terminal

$ curl -X PUT -d 'firstName=FOO&lastName=BAR&phone=12345678' http://localhost:80
80/contact/123
{"id":123,"firstName":"FOO","lastName":"BAR","phone":"12345678"}

$ ▮
```

If we want to see a verbose output that includes the request's and response's headers, we can use the `-v` (long name –verbose) flag. Also, in case we need to set the value of a request header, we can use the `-H` (long name –header) flag followed by the header information:

```
$ curl --header "Content-Type: application/json"
  http://localhost:8080/contact/1
```

Mapping the request data to representations

The current way of reading the web service properties by mentioning each one of them (annotated) in the signatures of the #createContact() and #updateContact() methods is fine; however, it is not efficient in case of significant amount of input data. Imagine a case where we would need to add several additional properties in the Contact class. We would have to also update the method signatures as well, making them less readable and finally unmanageable. Generally, it is preferred to map the request data to the representation directly. To achieve this, we will update the relevant methods accordingly, removing the properties and adding a contact instance instead. Jackson will take care of the rest.

How to do it...

Perform the following steps to map the request data:

1. Update the ContactResource#createContact() method, replacing its parameters with a single contact object:

    ```
    @POST
    public Response createContact(Contact contact) {
      // store the new contact
      // ...
      return Response
          .created(null)
          .build();
    }
    ```

2. Update the ContactResource#updateContact() method, replacing its parameters with a single contact object:

    ```
    @PUT
    @Path("/{id}")
    public Response updateContact(
        @PathParam("id") int id,
        Contact contact) {
      // update the contact with the provided ID
      // ...
      return Response
          .ok(new Contact(id, contact.getFirstName(), contact.
    getLastName(), contact.getPhone()))
          .build();
    }
    ```

3. Rebuild and run the application again. The application is now able to handle HTTP POST and PUT requests to the `/contact` and `/contact/{id}` endpoints respectively, having JSON strings on the request body instead of the named parameters. Note that the `Content-Type` header of the request will be set to `application/json`.

How it works...

By declaring a `Contact` instance as the parameter on a method that handles requests (that is, a method with Jersey annotations bound to URI), we force Jersey to parse the request body and deserialize (using Jackson) it to a `Contact` object.

The PUT request we performed in the previous example can now be performed by sending the JSON data to the server and setting the appropriate header, as shown in the following line of code:

```
$ curl --header "Content-Type: application/json" -X PUT -d
  '{"firstName": "FOO", "lastName":"BAR", "phone":"987654321"}'
  http://localhost:8080/contact/123
```

```
Terminal

$ curl --header "Content-Type: application/json" -X PUT -d '{"firstName": "FOO", "lastName":"BAR",
"phone":"987654321"}' http://localhost:8080/contact/123

{"id":123,"firstName":"FOO","lastName":"BAR","phone":"987654321"}

$
```

In case a POST request is performed on `http://localhost:8080/contact` with the `{"firstName": "Alexandros", "lastName": "Dallas", "phone": "+3012345678"}` JSON data as the request's body and the `Content-Type` header: `application/json`, the `contact` object within the `#createContact()` method will have its properties initialized accordingly, thanks to Jackson and its appropriate JAX-RS entity providers. Entity providers are components that process the payload that is included in an HTTP request and transform it to an object. This is similar to the transformation that happens when a `resource` method is returning an object and is transformed to a JSON object.

6
Using a Database

Our application is growing steadily. We now need a place to store the contacts we are going to manage, and an efficient way to do so. We will use the MySQL server, whose installation was outlined in the first chapter of the book, for our data storage needs. Dropwizard provides everything we will need to interact with it.

Preparing the database

It is time to actually store and retrieve data with our application. We are going to create a connection between our application and a MySQL database.

We will need an actual database to connect to and query. Since we have MySQL installed, we can also use the `mysql` command-line client in order to create a database and some tables in it.

Getting ready

Start the `mysql` client by executing the following command in your terminal:

```
$ mysql -u root -p
```

As shown in the following screenshot, the MySQL shell will then prompt you to provide your password, which is the password of the MySQL root user that you set during the installation of MySQL:

```
  ● — □   Terminal
$ mysql -u root -p
Enter password:
Welcome to the MySQL monitor.  Commands end with ; or \g.
Your MySQL connection id is 164
Server version: 5.5.31-0ubuntu0.12.04.1 (Ubuntu)

Copyright (c) 2000, 2013, Oracle and/or its affiliates. All rights reserved.

Oracle is a registered trademark of Oracle Corporation and/or its
affiliates. Other names may be trademarks of their respective
owners.

Type 'help;' or '\h' for help. Type '\c' to clear the current input statement.

mysql>
```

How to do it...

Let's follow the next steps in order to prepare our application's database:

1. Create the database phonebook by running the following query:

   ```
   > CREATE DATABASE `phonebook`;
   ```

2. We will need an additional MySQL user with full rights to the newly created database. Create the user and grant appropriate access rights with the following commands:

   ```
   > CREATE USER 'phonebookuser'@'localhost' IDENTIFIED BY
     'phonebookpassword';
   > GRANT ALL ON phonebook.* TO 'phonebookuser'@'localhost';
   ```

3. Select the phonebook database with the USE command:

   ```
   > USE `phonebook`;
   ```

4. Create the contact table in order to store some contacts.

   ```
   > CREATE TABLE IF NOT EXISTS `contact` (
       `id` int(11) NOT NULL AUTO_INCREMENT,
       `firstName` varchar(255) NOT NULL,
       `lastName` varchar(255) NOT NULL,
       `phone` varchar(30) NOT NULL,
       PRIMARY KEY (`id`)
       )
   ```

```
ENGINE=InnoDB

DEFAULT CHARSET=utf8

AUTO_INCREMENT=1 ;
```

5. Add some test data in the contact table:

```
> INSERT INTO `contact` VALUES (NUL L, 'John', 'Doe',
  '+123456789'), (NULL, 'Jane', 'Doe', '+987654321');
```

How it works...

We have just set up our database. With the queries we ran, we created a database along with a database user and a table to hold contact-related information. Our application will be updated in order to store and retrieve information to and from this table.

Interacting with the database

Now we have a database and data in place. However, in order to be able to connect to the database, we need to include the `mysql jdbc` connector in the project. Also, we will need the `dropwizard-jdbi` module that will allow us to create a database connection and **Data Access Objects** (**DAO**) through which we will query the database, making use of the API provided by the JDBI project (`http://jdbi.org/`).

Getting ready

Let's see what is needed in order to achieve this. First, add the following dependencies in `pom.xml` within the `<dependencies>` section:

```
<dependency>
  <groupId>mysql</groupId>
  <artifactId>mysql-connector-java</artifactId>
  <version>5.1.6</version>
</dependency>
<dependency>
  <groupId>io.dropwizard</groupId>
  <artifactId>dropwizard-jdbi</artifactId>
  <version>0.7.0-SNAPSHOT</version>
</dependency>
```

We are now ready to proceed and update our application. We are going to use JDBI's SQL object API mapping methods to predefine the SQL statements.

How to do it...

Let's see how to connect and interact with the database through our application by following the next steps:

1. Create a new package, `com.dwbook.phonebook.dao`, and a `ContactDAO` interface in it with the following code:

```
package com.dwbook.phonebook.dao;
public interface ContactDAO { }
```

2. Add the `#getContactById()` method, which will allow us to query the database and retrieve a list of contacts or a specific contact when its ID is given. Use the `@SqlQuery` annotation to specify the SQL query that will be executed when the method is called. You will need to import `org.skife.jdbi.v2.sqlobject.*` and `com.dwbook.phonebook.representations.Contact`.

```
@SqlQuery("select * from contact where id = :id")
Contact getContactById(@Bind("id") int id);
```

3. Create a `com.dwbook.phonebook.dao.mappers` package and the `ContactMapper` class that implements the map method, as shown in the following code snippet. Mapper classes facilitate the mapping of a `resultset` database row to an object. You will need to import `java.sql.ResultSet`, `java.sql.SQLException`, `org.skife.jdbi.v2.StatementContext`, `org.skife.jdbi.v2.tweak.ResultSetMapper`, and `com.dwbook.phonebook.representations.Contact`.

```
public class ContactMapper implements ResultSetMapper<Contact>
{
    public Contact map(int index, ResultSet r,
      StatementContext ctx)
    throws SQLException {
    return new Contact(
    r.getInt("id"), r.getString("firstName"),
    r.getString("lastName"),r.getString("phone"));
    }
}
```

4. In `ContactDAO`, register your mapper with the `#getContactById()` method by adding the `@Mapper` annotation to it (before the `@SqlQuery` annotation). Import the `com.dwbook.phonebook.dao.mappers.ContactMapper` and `org.skife.jdbi.v2.sqlobject.customizers.Mapper` classes.

```
@Mapper(ContactMapper.class)
@SqlQuery("select * from contact where id = :id")
Contact getContactById(@Bind("id") int id);
```

5. In the `config.yaml` configuration file, add the section database consisting of the minimum set of properties required for establishing a database connection (indented according to the `YAML` syntax).

```
database:
    driverClass: com.mysql.jdbc.Driver
    user: phonebookuser
    password: phonebookpassword
    url: jdbc:mysql://localhost/phonebook
```

6. Add the database property in the `PhonebookConfiguration` class, and create a getter method for it. Import the `io.dropwizard.db.DataSourceFactory` class first.

```
@JsonProperty
private DataSourceFactory database = new
  DataSourceFactory();


  public DataSourceFactory getDataSourceFactory() {
      return database;
  }
}
```

7. Modify the `run` method in the `App` class in order to create a DBIFactory class that will be used to build a `DBI` instance, which we will then pass as a parameter to `ContactResource`. You will need to import `org.skife.jdbi.v2.DBI` and `io.dropwizard.jdbi.DBIFactory`.

```
@Override
public void run(PhonebookConfiguration c, Environment e)
  throws Exception {
  LOGGER.info("Method App#run() called");
  for (int i=0; i < c.getMessageRepetitions(); i++) {
    System.out.println(c.getMessage());
  }
  System.out.println(c.getAdditionalMessage());

  // Create a DBI factory and build a JDBI instance
  final DBIFactory factory = new DBIFactory();
  final DBI jdbi = factory
    .build(e, c.getDataSourceFactory(), "mysql");
  // Add the resource to the environment
  e.jersey().register(new ContactResource(jdbi));
}
```

8. In the previous step, we passed the `jdbi` instance as a parameter to the `ContactResource` constructor. However, the constructor `ContactResource(DBI)` does not exist (yet), so we need to create it. We will add a private final `ContactDAO` member in our resource class using the `onDemand` method and use JDBI to instantiate it. You will also need to add the necessary imports for `DBI` and `ContactDAO`.

```
private final ContactDAO contactDao;
  public ContactResource(DBI jdbi) {
  contactDao = jdbi.onDemand(ContactDAO.class);
}
```

9. Modify the `ContactResource#getContact()` method class using the `contactDao` object so it returns an actual contact from the database.

```
@GET
@Path("/{id}")
public Response getContact(@PathParam("id") int id) {
  // retrieve information about the contact with the
    provided id
  Contact contact = contactDao.getContactById(id);
  return Response
    .ok(contact)
    .build();
}
```

10. Rebuild and run the application, providing the updated configuration file as an argument.

11. Open your browser and go to `http://localhost:8080/contact/1`. You will see a JSON representation of the first row we inserted in the contact table, the one having `id` equal to 1, that is, `John Doe`. Take a look at the following screenshot which outlines this:

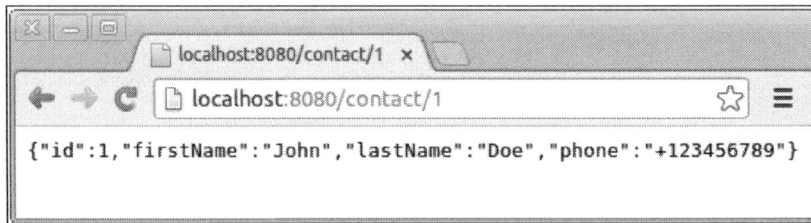

Respectively, the following screenshot shows the output for `http://localhost:8080/contact/2`:

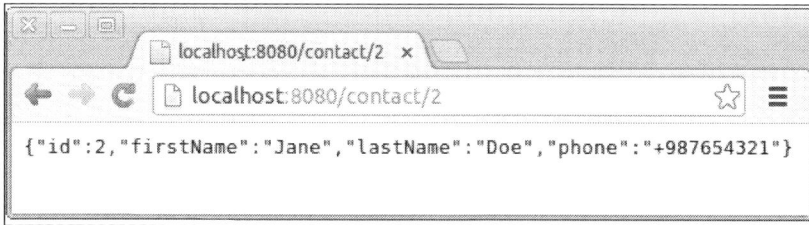

```
{"id":2,"firstName":"Jane","lastName":"Doe","phone":"+987654321"}
```

12. Now, let's add the methods for creating, updating, and deleting contacts in our DAO. For inserting new entries, add the `#createContact()` method.

```
@GetGeneratedKeys
@SqlUpdate("insert into contact (id, firstName, lastName,
    phone) values (NULL, :firstName, :lastName, :phone)")
int createContact(@Bind("firstName") String firstName,
    @Bind("lastName") String lastName, @Bind("phone")
    String phone);
```

> Note that since we are updating the database and not querying it (that is, retrieving information), we use the `@SqlUpdate` annotation for the SQL query instead of the `@SqlQuery` annotation we used in the `#getContact()` method. Also, the `@GetGeneratedKeys` annotation is used in order to retrieve the value of the primary key of the newly inserted row; in this case, the value of the `id` field.

13. For updating existing entries, add the `#updateContact()` method:

```
@SqlUpdate("update contact set firstName = :firstName, lastName =
:lastName, phone = :phone where id = :id")
void updateContact(@Bind("id") int id, @Bind("firstName")
    String firstName, @Bind("lastName") String
    lastName,@Bind("phone") String phone);
```

14. In order to delete existing entries, add the `#deleteContact()` method:

```
@SqlUpdate("delete from contact where id = :id")
void deleteContact(@Bind("id") int id);
```

15. Now that we have the database methods in place, let's use them in the `Resource` class so that we actually insert, update, and delete contacts. Modify the `ContactResource#createContact()` method in order to insert the new contact in the database, retrieve its `id`, and use it to construct its URI, passing it as a parameter to the `Response#created()` method. For this, we will need to import `java.net.URI` and `java.net.URISyntaxException` first:

```
@POST
public Response createContact(Contact contact) throws
  URISyntaxException {
  // store the new contact
  int newContactId =
    contactDao.createContact(contact.getFirstName(),
    contact.getLastName(), contact.getPhone());
  return Response.created(new
    URI(String.valueOf(newContactId))).build();
}
```

16. In a similar way, update the `ContactResource#deleteContact()` method so that the contacts can indeed be deleted:

```
@DELETE
@Path("/{id}")
public Response deleteContact(@PathParam("id") int id) {
  // delete the contact with the provided id
  contactDao.deleteContact(id);
  return Response.noContent().build();
}
```

17. Finally, let's also update the `ContactResource#updateContact()` method so that our application can update existing contacts while handling the relevant HTTP requests:

```
@PUT
@Path("/{id}")
public Response updateContact(@PathParam("id") int id,
  Contact contact) {
  // update the contact with the provided ID
  contactDao.updateContact(id, contact.getFirstName(),
    contact.getLastName(), contact.getPhone());
  return Response.ok(
    new Contact(id, contact.getFirstName(),
      contact.getLastName(),
        contact.getPhone())).build();
}
```

How it works...

Thanks to JDBI, our phonebook application can now interact with a database, retrieving, storing, updating, and deleting contacts.

Let's create a new contact by performing an HTTP POST request with `curl`.

```
$ curl --verbose --header "Content-Type: application/json" -X POST
  -d '{"firstName": "FOO", "lastName":"BAR", "phone":"987654321"}'
  http://localhost:8080/contact/
```

The contact is created, and the value of the inserted row's primary key, that is, the contact id, is 174, as you can see (the `Location` response header) in the following screenshot:

JDBI's SQL Object API simplifies the creation of DAO. We created the DAO interfaces on which we can map plain, parameterized SQL queries to specific methods using the `@SqlQuery` annotation; note that apart from the object mapper, no additional implementation is needed.

Since we are retrieving data from the database and returning a `Contact` instance, we needed to create a `Mapper` class, which is a class that implements the `org.skife.jdbi.v2.tweak.ResultSetMapper<T>` interface for the `Contact` class. Its implementation was fairly simple and straightforward. We created a `Contact` object with the values we got from the database `ResultSet` object using the `#getLong()` and `#getString()` methods and providing the column name.

We used `jdbi` to create our DAO instances within our resource class using the `DBI#onDemand()` method. However, in order to do that, we had to create a `DBI` factory and build the `DBI` instance prior to registering our resources. Again, this was pretty simple, and required minor modifications in the `App#run()` method.

The `DBI` factory requires the database connection settings in order to build the `DBI` instance. Going one step back, we had our configuration class updated to read and expose the `DatabaseConfiguration` settings, which were declared in the database section of the applications configuration file, that is, `config.yaml`.

There's more...

JDBI identifies itself as an SQL convenience library for Java. We used the JDBI SQL Object API where a particular method is mapped to a specific SQL statement. However, this is not the only way of using JDBI to interact with a database. JDBI exposes another API too, that is, the fluent style API.

The JDBI fluent style API

The fluent style API allows us to open and use a database handle to create and execute SQL queries on demand on the fly, instead of using the predefined SQL statements that the SQL Object API utilizes.

Generally, the type of API that you should use depends on your personal taste, and you can even mix both APIs together.

The @MapResultAsBean annotation

In this example, we have implemented a mapper and used the `@Mapper` annotation in order to map the result of an SQL query to a `Contact` instance. An alternative approach would be the use of the `MapResultAsBean` annotation.

```
@MapResultAsBean
@SqlQuery("select * from contact where id = :id")
Contact getContactById(@Bind("id") int id);
```

By annotating `#getContactById()` in this example, we map the result of the SQL query directly to a `Contact` instance, without needing to implement a custom mapper. In order for this to work though, the `Contact` class should be updated with setters (that is, `setFirstName(String firstName) { .. }`). Due to this, the final keyword will have to be removed from the declaration of each member variable.

7

Validating Web Service Requests

Up to this point, we have a RESTful Web Service that produces JSON representations and is also capable of storing and updating contacts. Before we actually store or update a contact's information though, we need to ensure that the provided information is valid and consistent.

Adding validation constraints

The first thing we need to do in order to validate contacts is to define what is considered a valid contact. To do so, we will modify the representation class, adding constraints to its members in the form of Hibernate Validator annotations.

How to do it...

We have the `Contact` class, instances of which must have a first name, a last name, and a phone number in order to be considered valid. Moreover, the length of these values must be within specific limits. Let's go through the required steps in order to apply these constraints.

Modify the `Contact` representation class, adding the appropriate annotations to its members (import `org.hibernate.validator.constraints.*` first):

1. Update the declaration of the `firstName` variable, adding the necessary annotations in order to indicate that this is a required property (it should not be blank), and its length should be between 2 and 255 characters.

   ```
   @NotBlank
   @Length(min=2, max=255)
   private final String firstName;
   ```

2. In a similar way, apply the same constraints on the `lastName` property.

```
@NotBlank
@Length(min=2, max=255)
private final String lastName;
```

3. The `phone` field should not be longer than 30 digits, so modify the values of the relevant annotation accordingly.

```
@NotBlank
@Length(min=2, max=30)
private final String phone;
```

How it works...

The declaration of validation constraints is annotation-based. This gives us the flexibility of directly adding the validation rules we want to the members of our representation class.

Hibernate Validator is a part of the `dropwizard-core` module, so we do not need to declare any additional dependencies on our `pom.xml`.

There's more...

The recommended way of validating objects is using the standard **Bean Validation API** (**JSR 303**). For our validation needs, we use **Hibernate Validator**, which is a part of the `Dropwizard-core` module, and the reference implementation of JSR 303. Using Hibernate Validator, we can declare field constraints such as `@NotBlank` and `@Length`, or even create and use our own custom constraints that fit our needs (you may refer to Hibernate Validator's documentation at `http://docs.jboss.org/hibernate/stable/validator/reference/en-US/html_single/#validator-customconstraints`).

List of constraint annotations

The complete list of field constraints is available on the Hibernate Validator package navigator at `http://docs.jboss.org/hibernate/stable/validator/reference/en-US/html_single/#section-builtin-constraints`.

Performing validation

We've just defined what a valid annotation is. Now, we must modify the code of our resource class in order to verify that each POST and PUT request contains a valid `Contact` object, based on which a contact is created or updated.

How to do it...

Let's see what needs to be modified in our resource class by performing the following steps:

1. First, we need to import some classes that will help us with the validation.

```
import java.util.Set;
import javax.validation.ConstraintViolation;
import javax.util.ArrayList;
import javax.validation.Validator;
import javax.ws.rs.core.Response.Status;
```

2. Add a final member, `validator`, and update the constructor method in order to initialize it.

```
private final ContactDAO contactDao;  private final Validator
validator;
    public ContactResource(DBI jdbi, Validator validator) {
      contactDao = jdbi.onDemand(ContactDAO.class);      this.
validator = validator;
    }
```

3. In the `App` class, modify the `#run()` method so as to pass the environment's `validator` as a parameter to `ContactResource` during its initialization, along with jDBI.

```
// …
// Add the resource to the environment
e.jersey().register(new ContactResource(jdbi, e.getValidator()));
// …
```

4. Update the `ContactResource#createContact()` method and check that the contact information is valid prior to inserting it in the database.

```
@POST
public Response createContact(Contact contact) throws
  URISyntaxException {
  // Validate the contact's data
  Set<ConstraintViolation<Contact>> violations =
    validator.validate(contact);
  // Are there any constraint violations?
  if (violations.size() > 0) {
    // Validation errors occurred
    ArrayList<String> validationMessages = new
      ArrayList<String>();
```

```
        for (ConstraintViolation<Contact> violation :
            violations) {
validationMessages.add(violation.getPropertyPath().toString() +":
" + violation.getMessage());
        }
      return Response
            .status(Status.BAD_REQUEST)
            .entity(validationMessages)
            .build();
    }
    else {
      // OK, no validation errors
      // Store the new contact
      int newContactId =
        contactDao.createContact(contact.getFirstName(),
        contact.getLastName(), contact.getPhone());
      return Response.created(new
        URI(String.valueOf(newContactId))).build();
    }
  }
```

5. Similarly, update the `ContactResource#updateContact()` method.

```
@PUT
@Path("/{id}")
public Response updateContact(@PathParam("id") int id,
  Contact contact) {
  // Validate the updated data
  Set<ConstraintViolation<Contact>> violations =
    validator.validate(contact);
  // Are there any constraint violations?
  if (violations.size() > 0) {
    // Validation errors occurred
    ArrayList<String> validationMessages = new
      ArrayList<String>();
    for (ConstraintViolation<Contact> violation :
    violations) {
validationMessages.add(violation.getPropertyPath().toString() +":
" + violation.getMessage());
    }
    return Response
          .status(Status.BAD_REQUEST)
          .entity(validationMessages)
          .build();
  }
```

```
      else {
        // No errors
        // update the contact with the provided ID
        contactDao.updateContact(id, contact.getFirstName(),
            contact.getLastName(), contact.getPhone());
        return Response.ok(
            new Contact(id, contact.getFirstName(),
              contact.getLastName(),
            contact.getPhone())).build();
      }
    }
```

6. Build and run the application from the command line in order to do some tests with the validation mechanisms we just implemented.

7. Using `curl`, perform an HTTP POST request to `http://localhost:8080/contact/`, sending contact information that is going to trigger validation errors, such as `firstName` and `lastName` with length less than 2 characters, and an empty value for the `phone` field in a JSON string such as the following:

```
{"firstName": "F", "lastName": "L", "phone": ""}.
#> curl -v -X POST -d '{"firstName": "F", "lastName": "L",
   "phone": ""}' http://localhost:8080/contact/ --header
   "Content-Type: application/json"
```

```
$ curl -v -X POST -d '{"firstName": "F", "lastName": "L", "phone": ""}' http://localhost:8080/contact/
--header "Content-Type: application/json"
* About to connect() to localhost port 8080 (#0)
*   Trying 127.0.0.1... connected
> POST /contact/ HTTP/1.1
> User-Agent: curl/7.22.0 (i686-pc-linux-gnu) libcurl/7.22.0 OpenSSL/1.0.1 zlib/1.2.3.4 libidn/1.23 lib
rtmp/2.3
> Host: localhost:8080
> Accept: */*
> Content-Type: application/json
> Content-Length: 48
>
* upload completely sent off: 48out of 48 bytes
< HTTP/1.1 400 Bad Request
< Date: Tue, 28 Jan 2014 20:16:57 GMT
< Content-Type: application/json
< Transfer-Encoding: chunked
<
* Connection #0 to host localhost left intact
* Closing connection #0
["phone: length must be between 2 and 30","firstName: length must be between 2 and 255","lastName: leng
th must be between 2 and 255","phone: may not be empty"]
$
```

You will see that the response is an **HTTP/1.1 400 Bad Request** error, and the response payload is a JSON array containing the following error messages:

```
< HTTP/1.1 400 Bad Request

< Date: Tue, 28 Jan 2014 20:16:57 GMT

< Content-Type: application/json

< Transfer-Encoding: chunked

<

* Connection #0 to host localhost left intact

* Closing connection #0

[
  "phone: length must be between 2 and 30",
  "firstName: length must be between 2 and 255",
  "lastName: length must be between 2 and 255",
  "phone: may not be empty"
]
```

How it works...

In the `ContactResource#createContact()` method, which is mapped to the POST requests to `/contact` URI, we used the environment's instance of `javax.validation.Validator` to validate the received `contact` object.

The validator's `#validate()` method returns a `Set<ConstraintViolation<Contact>>` instance, which contains the validation error that occurred, if any. We check the list's size to determine if there are any violations. If there are, we will iterate through them, extracting the validation message of each error and adding it to an `ArrayList` instance, which we then return as a response along with **HTTP Status Code 400 – Bad Request**.

Since our resource class produces a JSON output (already declared with the `@Produces` annotation at the class level), the `ArrayList` instance will be transformed to a JSON array thanks to Jackson.

There's more...

As you saw, in order to test and showcase the POST requests to the endpoint we created, we need an HTTP client. Apart from cURL, there are some really good and useful HTTP client tools available (such as Postman for Google Chrome, available at `https://chrome.google.com/webstore/detail/postman-rest-client/fdmmgilgnpjigdojojpjoooidkmcomcm`) that can help us with this, and we will also create our own in the next chapter.

The @Valid annotation

Instead of using a `validator` object to validate the input object, we could have just annotated the `contact` object as `@Valid` on the `#createContact` method, as seen in the following line of code:

```
public Response createContact(@Valid Contact contact)
```

When an object is annotated with `@Valid`, the validation is recursively performed on it. This would have the validation triggered as soon as the method was called. In case the `contact` object was found invalid, then a default **HTTP 422 – Unprocessable entity** response will be generated automatically. While the `validator` object is more powerful and customizable, the usage of the `@Valid` annotation is an alternative, simple, and straightforward way to validate incoming requests. This prevents the need to return a custom, more descriptive validation error message to the caller, and sends a generic one instead.

Cross-field validation

There are cases where validation should be performed on multiple fields (properties) of an object. We can achieve this by implementing custom validation annotations that also apply class-level constraints.

Luckily enough, there's a much simpler way to achieve this. Dropwizard offers the `io.dropwizard.validation.ValidationMethod` annotation, which we can use in a `boolean` method of our representation class.

How to do it...

Here are the steps needed in order to add cross-field validation to a `contact` object. We will check that the contact's full name is not John Doe:

1. Add a new method in the `Contact` class named `#isValidPerson()`.

    ```
    public boolean isValidPerson() {
      if (firstName.equals("John") && lastName.equals("Doe")) {
        return false;
      }
    ```

```
        else {
          return true;
        }
    }
```

2. Then, we need to ensure that the output of this method will never be included in the output when it is serialized by Jackson. For this, annotate the `#isValidPerson()` method with the `@JsonIgnore` annotation (`com.fasterxml.jackson. annotation.JsonIgnore`).

3. Finally, annotate the same method with `@ValidationMethod` (`io.dropwizard. validation.ValidationMethod`), and also provide an error message in case of validation failure.

```
@ValidationMethod(message="John Doe is not a valid
    person!")
```

How it works...

When the validation is triggered, the `#isValidPerson()` method is executed along with the custom validation code we've put there. If the method returns true, that means the constraint implied by it is satisfied. If the method returns false, that indicates a constraint violation, and the validation error message will be the one we specified along with the `ValidationMethod` annotation.

You can create and have as many cross-field validation methods as you want in your classes. However, note that every custom validation method must be of the return type `boolean`, and its name must begin with `is`.

The Web Service Client

8

We have our service ready and functional, but we need an interface to actually use it. Of course, by using a web browser, we are able to perform HTTP GET requests, but not more complex requests such as POST. We need to create an HTTP Client for that.

Also, in many cases, you may need to have your web services call other web services and then perform additional processing before returning information to the caller.

Building a client for our application

Dropwizard includes both Jersey and Apache HTTP clients. We will use the Jersey client to create a client for our web service.

Getting ready

Add the `dropwizard-client` module to the dependencies section of your `pom.xml` in order to add web service client support to our project:

```
<dependency>
  <groupId>io.dropwizard</groupId>
  <artifactId>dropwizard-client</artifactId>
  <version>0.7.0-SNAPSHOT</version>
</dependency>
```

How to do it...

We will create a new resource class that will listen for and accept HTTP GET requests from our web browser and then call the appropriate method of the `Contact` resource and render the response in a human-friendly format. Let's have a look at the steps required in order to achieve this:

1. Create the `ClientResource` class in the `com.dwbook.phonebook.resources` package. Similar to the `ContactResource` class, we should first import the required `javax.ws.rs` annotations, the representation classes we are going to use, as well as the required Jersey client classes as shown in the following code snippet:

    ```
    package com.dwbook.phonebook.resources;

    import javax.ws.rs.*;
    import javax.ws.rs.core.*;
    import com.dwbook.phonebook.representations.Contact;
    import com.sun.jersey.api.client.*;

    public class ClientResource { }
    ```

2. Set the context path of the client resource class to `/client/` to logically separate the URIs of client and service by adding the appropriate annotation to the newly created class:

    ```
    @Path("/client/")
    public class ClientResource { }
    ```

3. Since our client is going to be used by humans, we need a human-friendly response type such as `text/plain`, so we will use `MediaType.TEXT_PLAIN`. Define it by adding the `@Produces` annotation to our class.

    ```
    @Produces(MediaType.TEXT_PLAIN)
    @Path("/client/")
    public class ClientResource { }
    ```

4. In order to perform calls to other web services (in this case, our service, the `ContactResource` class), we need to have a `Client` instance as a member of our resource class. This will be provided during initialization, so we need to have an appropriate constructor.

    ```
    private Client client;
      public ClientResource(Client client) {
        this.client = client;
      }
    ```

5. Instantiate the client in our application's entry class, and also add the new resource to the environment by adding a couple of lines of code to the App#run() method. Of course, we first need to import `com.sun.jersey.api.client.Client`, `io.dropwizard.client.JerseyClientBuilder`, and the `com.dwbook.phonebook.resources.ClientResource` class we've just created.

    ```
    // build the client and add the resource to the
       environment
    final Client client = new
      JerseyClientBuilder(e).build("REST Client");
    e.jersey().register(new ClientResource(client));
    ```

How it works...

We now have the client resource ready. This resource has a Jersey `Client` object as a member, which we can use to perform HTTP requests on specific URLs by building `WebResource` objects (using the `Client#resource()` method) and interacting with them.

There's more...

Most of the time, and generally in large-scale applications, the client is decoupled from the backend services, forming a separate application. Backend services usually perform more intensive and complex tasks, and it is generally a good practice to treat and scale them independently from the client.

Interacting with our services

We will proceed by adding the necessary methods to the `ClientResource` class, bound to the GET requests so they can be easily triggered with a browser. We need to add methods for creating, updating, deleting, and retrieving contacts, which we will trigger by performing appropriate HTTP requests.

How to do it...

1. Add the `#showContact()` method to the `ClientResource` class, binding the query `String` parameter `id` as the input using the `@QueryParam` annotation.

    ```
    @GET
    @Path("showContact")
    public String showContact(@QueryParam("id") int id) {
      WebResource contactResource =
        client.resource("http://localhost:8080/contact/"+id);
      Contact c = contactResource.get(Contact.class);
      String output = "ID: "+ id
          +"\nFirst name: " + c.getFirstName()
          + "\nLast name: " + c.getLastName()
          + "\nPhone: " + c.getPhone();
      return output;
    }
    ```

2. Create the `#newContact()` method. This method is going to accept the properties of a `Contact` object as parameters and will create a new contact by performing the appropriate HTTP request to the `ContactResource` service.

    ```
    @GET
    @Path("newContact")
    ```

```
    public Response newContact(@QueryParam("firstName")
      String firstName, @QueryParam("lastName") String
      lastName, @QueryParam("phone") String phone) {
      WebResource contactResource =
        client.resource("http://localhost:8080/contact");
      ClientResponse response = contactResource.type(MediaType.
APPLICATION_JSON).post(ClientResponse.class, new Contact(0,
firstName, lastName, phone));
      if (response.getStatus() == 201) {
        // Created
        return Response.status(302).entity("The contact was
         created successfully! The new contact can be found
         at " +
         response.getHeaders().getFirst("Location")).build();
      }
      else {
        // Other Status code, indicates an error
        return Response.status(422).entity(response.
getEntity(String.class)).build();
      }
    }
```

3. The `#updateContact()` method for updating contacts will be quite similar to the previous one.

```
@GET
  @Path("updateContact")
  public Response updateContact(@QueryParam("id") int id,
    @QueryParam("firstName") String firstName,
    @QueryParam("lastName") String lastName,
    @QueryParam("phone") String phone) {
    WebResource contactResource =
      client.resource("http://localhost:8080/contact/" +
      id);
    ClientResponse response = contactResource.type(MediaType.
APPLICATION_JSON).put(ClientResponse.class, new Contact(id,
firstName, lastName, phone));
      if (response.getStatus() == 200) {
        // Created
        return Response.status(302).entity("The contact was
          updated successfully!").build();
      }
      else {
        // Other Status code, indicates an error
        return Response.status(422).entity(response.
getEntity(String.class)).build();
      }
    }
```

4. In a similar way, let's add the method for deleting contacts, `#deleteContact()`.

```
@GET
  @Path("deleteContact")
  public Response deleteContact(@QueryParam("id") int id) {
    WebResource contactResource =
      client.resource("http://localhost:8080/contact/"+id);
    contactResource.delete();
    return Response.noContent().entity("Contact was
      deleted!").build();
  }
```

5. Now you may build and run the application in order to see what we've done up to this point.

How it works...

Point your browser at `http://localhost:8080/client/showContact?id=1`. The client will perform an HTTP GET request to `http://localhost:8080/contact/1`, parse the JSON representation of the contact, and produce a plain text summary of it.

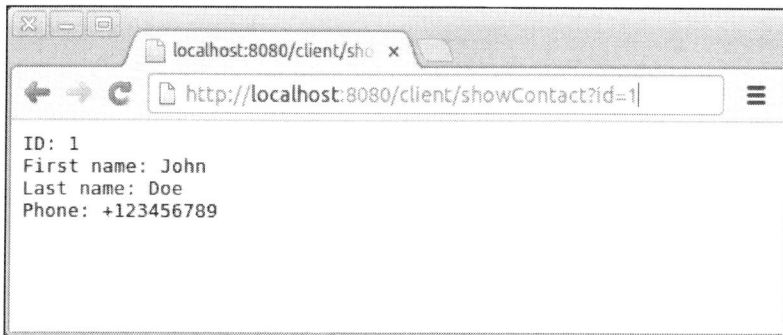

In order to perform an HTTP request, we must first create a `WebResource` instance (since RESTful Web Services are all about resources and HTTP verbs) using the `#resource(String)` method of our client. Think of `WebResource` as a proxy for a specific web service endpoint.

The `#get()` method of the `WebResource` class takes the class that we will use to parse and map the response as a parameter, which will also be its return type.

For the HTTP POST request though, we use the generic HTTP response class, `ClientResponse`, which we can use to extract the status code of the response using the `#getStatus()` method. Also, we can extract its headers using the `#getHeaders()` method.

Note that for POST and PUT requests, we are also setting up the media type of the request data (`WebResource#type()`).

If you point your web browser at `http://localhost:8080/client/newContact?f irstName=Jane&lastName=Doe&phone=98765432`, our client will post that data to `ClientResource`, which will create a new contact and return its location back to the client. The client will then show us the new contact's URL as seen in the following screenshot:

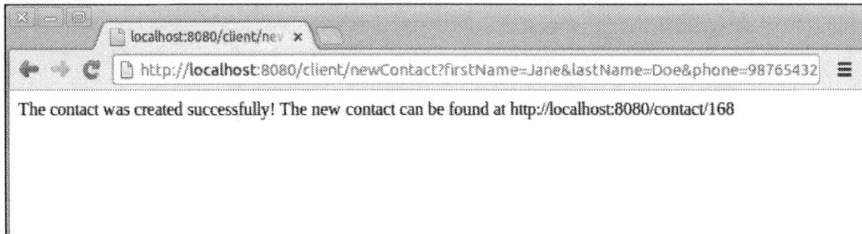

Similarly, we can update a contact using the client by requesting the appropriate URL. The URL `http://localhost:8080/client/updateContact?id=1&firstName=Ale x&lastName=Updated&phone=3210465` will trigger a PUT request to the contact service, which will eventually update the contact with `id` equal to 1.

As you may already be guessing, the URL `http://localhost:8080/client/ deleteContact?id=1` will send the relevant HTTP DELETE request to contact service, deleting the contact identified by the given `id`.

There's more...

Note that in the case of validation errors during the creation of a new contact, these errors are communicated to the client. Our client checks the status code of the POST request, and if it is not equal to `201` (which indicates that the entity has been created), then it parses the response as a string and presents it to the user.

For example, navigate to `http://localhost:8080/client/newContact?firstNam e=J&lastName=D&phone=9`. Since we have set constraints indicating that the length of `firstName`, `lastName`, and `phone` shall be greater than 2, we will get validation errors as you can see in the following screenshot:

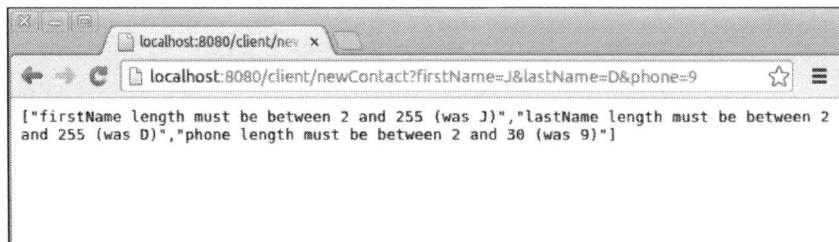

9
Authentication

Authentication is the process of verifying that the user who is accessing an application is indeed who he/she claims to be and also, that he/she is allowed to access and use our application. In this chapter, we'll see how we can secure our web services with authentication mechanisms.

Building a basic HTTP authenticator

Our web service now has the functionality that allows anyone to use an HTTP client and create and retrieve contacts. We need to somehow secure our web service and authenticate the users that call it. The most common way of authentication is basic HTTP authentication, which requires a basic set of credentials: a username and password.

Getting ready

Before we proceed with securing our web service, we need to add the `dropwizard-auth` dependency to our project, adding the following to the dependencies section of our `pom.xml` file:

```xml
<dependency>
  <groupId>io.dropwizard</groupId>
  <artifactId>dropwizard-auth</artifactId>
  <version>0.7.0-SNAPSHOT</version>
</dependency>
```

How to do it...

Let's see what it takes to build the authentication mechanism and secure our methods; perform the following steps:

1. Create a new class in the `com.dwbook.phonebook` package named `PhonebookAuthenticator`; here, we are going to build our service's security mechanism. The class needs to implement the `Authenticator<C, P>` interface and its `#authenticate()` method. The first parameter of the authenticator is the `Authentication` method, whereas the second one is the return type of the `#authenticate()` method.

```
package com.dwbook.phonebook;
import com.google.common.base.Optional;
import io.dropwizard.auth.AuthenticationException;
import io.dropwizard.auth.Authenticator;
import io.dropwizard.auth.basic.BasicCredentials;
public class PhonebookAuthenticator implements
   Authenticator<BasicCredentials, Boolean> {
   public Optional<Boolean> authenticate(BasicCredentials
      c) throws AuthenticationException {
      if (c.getUsername().equals("john_doe") &&
        c.getPassword().equals("secret")) {
      return Optional.of(true);
      }
      return Optional.absent();
   }
}
```

2. Enable the authenticator you've just built by adding it to the Dropwizard environment along with `JerseyEnvironment#register()`, passing to it a `BasicAuthProvider` instance. The constructor of `BasicAuthProvider` takes an instance of the authenticator to be used as the input and the authentication realm. You will also need to import `io.dropwizard.auth.basic.BasicAuthProvider`.

```
// Register the authenticator with the environment
e.jersey().register(new BasicAuthProvider<Boolean>(
   new PhonebookAuthenticator(), "Web Service Realm"));
```

3. You may now secure web service endpoints, modifying the declarations of the `ContactResource` class' methods to expect a `Boolean` variable as the parameter, annotated with `@Auth` (import `io.dropwizard.auth.Auth`). The inclusion of this annotated parameter will trigger the authentication process.

```
public Response getContact(@PathParam("id") int id, @Auth
  Boolean isAuthenticated) { … }


public Response createContact(Contact contact, @Auth   Boolean
isAuthenticated) throws URISyntaxException { … }


public Response deleteContact(@PathParam("id") int id,
  @Auth Boolean isAuthenticated) { … }
public Response updateContact(@PathParam("id") int id,
  Contact contact, @Auth Boolean isAuthenticated) { … }
```

4. Build and start the application and then try to access any of the endpoints of the `ContactResource` class, such as `http://localhost:8080/contact/1`, trying to display the contact with an ID equal to 1. You will see a message stating that the server requires a username and a password.

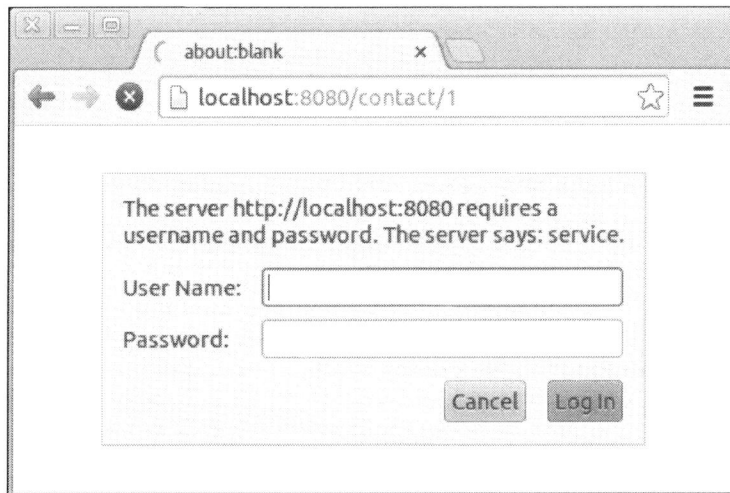

How it works...

The `dropwizard-auth` module includes everything we need in order to secure our services. We just need to implement an Authenticator and register it with the Dropwizard environment.

Then, when we use the `@Auth` annotation for a method's input parameter, we indicate that the user who is accessing our service must be authenticated. Each time an HTTP request is performed on a method that contains a variable annotated with `@Auth`, the authentication provider intercepts it requesting a username and password. These credentials are then passed on to our authenticator who is responsible for determining whether they're valid or not. Whatever the authentication result is, that is, the return value of the `#authenticate()` method, it is injected in the variable that is annotated with `@Auth`. In case the authentication is unsuccessful or no credentials are provided, the request is blocked and the response is an **HTTP/1.1 401 Unauthorized** error. You can see the response received after performing an HTTP request with cURL without providing credentials in the following screenshot:

```
⊗ ⊖ ◻   Terminal
>
< HTTP/1.1 401 Unauthorized
< Date: Tue, 28 Jan 2014 21:56:09 GMT
< WWW-Authenticate: Basic realm="Web Service Realm"
< Content-Type: text/plain
< Transfer-Encoding: chunked
<
* Connection #0 to host localhost left intact
* Closing connection #0
Credentials are required to access this resource.
$ 
```

Our authenticator class needs to be a class that implements the `Authenticator<C, P>` interface, where `C` is the set of credentials that we may use to authenticate the user and `P` is the type of the authentication's outcome. In our case, we used `BasicCredentials` as the credentials store, which is what `BasicAuthProvider` provides. In the `#authenticate()` method, we perform all the tasks required to authenticate the user. We implemented this to check that the user's name is `john_doe` as identified by the password, `secret`. This was an example; the next recipe illustrates how to authenticate users when their details (username and password) are stored in a database.

There's more...

As you may have noticed, our authenticator's `#authenticate()` method's return type is `Optional`. This is a Guava type that allows us to prevent null-pointer exceptions. There are cases where the `#authenticate()` method should return nothing, so instead of simply returning null (which could cause problems if not handled correctly), we return `Optional.absent()`.

Such cases are when we need to provide an instance of the authenticated principal (that would probably contain username, name, e-mail, and so on) to the methods we secure, instead of just a `boolean` parameter, as we did in this example.

Setting client's credentials

We have secured our web service, in particular the endpoints of the `ContactResource` class. Our client needs to be updated as well in order to be able to access these protected resources.

To do so, we will need to modify the `App#run()` method. Use the `#addFilter()` method of the `client` object, right after its instantiation, adding `HTTPBasicAuthFilter` (import `com.sun.jersey.api.client.filter.HTTPBasicAuthFilter`) and providing the correct username and password.

```
final Client client = new
  JerseyClientBuilder().using(environment).build();
  client.addFilter(new HTTPBasicAuthFilter("john_doe", "secret"));
```

The `#addFilter()` method is used to add additional processing instructions to the `client` object. That is, every request that is performed by our Jersey client has to be processed by the filters we've added before it is eventually performed. In this case, we use the `#addFilter()` method in order to add the appropriate `BasicAuth` headers to every outgoing HTTP request.

Optional authentication

There are many cases where authentication should be optional. Think of a service that returns personalized information for a user and a default message when no user is logged in. In order to declare optional authentication, we should have provided the `required=false` parameter on the `@Auth` annotation, as shown in the following code:

```
@Auth(required=false)
```

Authentication schemes

We used basic HTTP authentication in our application; however, it is not the only available authentication scheme. For example, some web services use API key authentication. In such cases, the authenticator should be checking the headers of the HTTP request, verifying the validity of the transmitted API key. However, doing so would require the usage of a custom authentication provider as well. In any case, the use of an authentication method depends on your application's needs.

Authenticating users with credentials stored in a database

In the previous recipe, we used a hard-coded set of username and password to verify the users' identity. In most real-world cases though, you will need to identify users and verify their identity using credentials that are stored in a database, or more specifically, in a table that holds user information.

Getting ready

Let's first create a table in the database that will hold user data.

Start the MySQL client, and after logging in, execute the following query in the phonebook database:

```
CREATE TABLE IF NOT EXISTS `users` (
  `username` varchar(20) NOT NULL,
  `password` varchar(255) NOT NULL,
  PRIMARY KEY (`username`)
) ENGINE=InnoDB DEFAULT CHARSET=utf8 AUTO_INCREMENT=1 ;
```

Now let's add a user to the database by running the following query:

```
INSERT INTO `users` VALUES ('wsuser', 'wspassword');
```

How to do it...

We are going to modify our authentication provider in order to check the current user's credentials in the database. Let's see how:

1. Since we are going to be interacting with the database for validating the user, we will need a DAO. So, create the UserDAO interface in the com.dwbook. phonebook.dao package.

   ```
   package com.dwbook.phonebook.dao;
   import org.skife.jdbi.v2.sqlobject.*;
   public interface UserDAO {
     @SqlQuery("select count(*) from users where username =
       :username and password = :password")
     int getUser(@Bind("username") String username,
       @Bind("password") String password);
   }
   ```

2. Modify `PhonebookAuthenticator`, adding a `UserDAO` instance as a member variable, creating a constructor to initialize the DAO instance using `jdbi`, and finally altering the authenticate method by utilizing the `UserDAO` instance for verifying user data by querying the database.

```
import org.skife.jdbi.v2.DBI;
import com.dwbook.phonebook.dao.UserDAO;
import com.google.common.base.Optional;
import
   io.dropwizard.auth.AuthenticationException;
import io.dropwizard.auth.Authenticator;
import io.dropwizard.auth.basic.BasicCredentials;

public class PhonebookAuthenticator implements
   Authenticator<BasicCredentials, Boolean> {
   private final UserDAO userDao;

   public PhonebookAuthenticator(DBI jdbi) {
     userDao = jdbi.onDemand(UserDAO.class);
   }

   public Optional<Boolean> authenticate(BasicCredentials
     c) throws AuthenticationException {
     boolean validUser = (userDao.getUser(c.getUsername(),
       c.getPassword()) == 1);
     if (validUser) {
       return Optional.of(true);
     }
     return Optional.absent();
   }
}
```

3. In the `App#run()` method, modify the registration of our authenticator in order to pass the existing `jdbi` instance to its constructor.

```
// Register the authenticator with the environment
e.jersey().register(new BasicAuthProvider<Boolean>(
   new PhonebookAuthenticator(jdbi), "Web Service Realm"));
```

You may now rebuild, run, and test the application again. This time, when requested, you will need to provide the username and password set stored in the database instead of the hard-coded ones.

How it works...

Upon every request that is performed on a protected resource, our application checks the user's credentials against the database. To do so, we created a simple DAO with a single query that actually counts the rows that match the provided username and password. Of course, this could be either 0 (when the username/password set is incorrect) or 1 (when there is a correct set of credentials provided). This is what we check for in the authenticator's `#authenticate()` method.

There's more...

In this recipe, we stored the password in a database as plain text. This is normally not the appropriate way to do so; passwords should always be encrypted or hashed, and never stored in clear text, to minimize the impact of a possible intrusion or unauthorized access.

Caching

To improve our application's performance, we could cache the database credentials. Dropwizard provides the `CachingAuthenticator` class that we could use for this matter. The concept is simple; we build a wrapper around our authenticator with the `CachingAuthenticator#wrap()` method and register it with the environment. We will also be defining a set of caching directives, for example, how many entries to cache and for how long, using Guava's `CacheBuilderSpec`. For this example, we need to import `io.dropwizard.auth.CachingAuthenticator` and `com.google.common.cache.CacheBuilderSpec`.

```
// Authenticator, with caching support (CachingAuthenticator)
CachingAuthenticator<BasicCredentials, Boolean> authenticator =
  new CachingAuthenticator<BasicCredentials, Boolean>(
e.metrics(),
new PhonebookAuthenticator(jdbi),
CacheBuilderSpec.parse("maximumSize=10000,
  expireAfterAccess=10m"));

// Register the authenticator with the environment
e.jersey().register(new BasicAuthProvider<Boolean>(
authenticator, "Web Service Realm"));

// Register the authenticator with the environment
e.jersey().register(new BasicAuthProvider<Boolean>(
authenticator, "Web Service Realm"));
```

The key statement in the preceding snippet is `CacheBuilderSpec.`
`parse("maximumSize=10000, expireAfterAccess=10m"));`. With this
statement, we configure the wrapper to cache `10000` principals (the `maximumSize`
property), that is, sets of usernames/passwords, and keep each of them cached for 10
minutes. The `CacheBuilderSpec#parse()` method is used to build a `CacheBuilderSpec`
instance by parsing a string. This is for our convenience, allowing us to externalize the cache
configuration, as instead of parsing a static string, we could parse a property defined in our
configuration settings file.

10
The User Interface – Views

Our web service client fetches information regarding a contact and presents it to the user as plain text. We are going to use Mustache, a template engine that is part of the `dropwizard-views-mustache` module, in order to create HTML views.

Building a user interface for the web service client

We will build a user interface for the web service client that consists of an HTML page that will be used to render a contact's details within a table.

Getting ready

Not surprisingly, the first thing we need to do is to add the `dropwizard-views` and `dropwizard-assets` dependencies in our `pom.xml`:

```xml
<dependency>
  <groupId>io.dropwizard</groupId>
  <artifactId>dropwizard-views-mustache</artifactId>
  <version>0.7.0-SNAPSHOT</version>
</dependency>
<dependency>
  <groupId>io.dropwizard</groupId>
  <artifactId>dropwizard-assets</artifactId>
  <version>0.7.0-SNAPSHOT</version>
</dependency>
```

Also, we will need to create a folder where we will store our template files. Create the [ProjectRoot]/src/main/resources/views folder as shown in the following screenshot:

How to do it...

1. Enable the Views bundle by adding it to your application's bootstrap in the #initialize() method of the App class. During the initialization phase (that is, when the #initialize() method is executed), we can use the bootstrap object to register additional modules with our application, such as bundles or commands. This has to be done before the service is actually started (that is, before the #run() method gets called). You will need to import io.dropwizard.views.ViewBundle:

```
@Override
public void initialize
    (Bootstrap<PhonebookConfiguration> b) {
      b.addBundle(new ViewBundle());
    }
```

2. Create a new package called com.dwbook.phonebook.views with the ContactView class in it. The class must extend View and its constructor will expect a Contact instance. Also, you must call the superclass's constructor specifying the template file for this class (in this case, contact.mustache, which is stored in the directory we created before). You can reference the view file using an absolute path, where the root is the [ProjectRoot]/src/main/resources/views folder. A getter for the contact object is needed so that it can be accessed by the template engine:

```
package com.dwbook.phonebook.views;

import com.dwbook.phonebook.representations.Contact;
import io.dropwizard.views.View;

public class ContactView extends View {
   private final Contact contact;

   public ContactView(Contact contact) {
```

```
        super("/views/contact.mustache");
        this.contact = contact;
    }

    public Contact getContact() {
        return contact;
    }
}
```

3. Now, let's create our template, `contact.moustache`, which will be a plain HTML file that renders a table with a contact's details. Remember to store it inside the `views` folder we created at the beginning. Take a look at the following code snippet:

```html
<html>
  <head>
    <title>Contact</title>
  </head>
  <body>
    <table border="1">
      <tr>
        <th colspan="2">Contact ({{contact.id}})</th>
      </tr>
      <tr>
        <td>First Name</td>
        <td>{{contact.firstName}}</td>
      </tr>
      <tr>
        <td>Last Name</td>
        <td>{{contact.lastName}}</td>
      </tr>
      <tr>
        <td>Phone</td>
        <td>{{contact.phone}}</td>
      </tr>
    </table>
  </body>
</html>
```

The Mustache tags, that is, the double-curly-braces-wrapped text, will be replaced with the actual values of the contact object's properties on runtime automatically. Mustache provides many tag types that you can use in your template, such as `conditionals` and `loops`. You may refer to `http://mustache.github.io/mustache.5.html` for detailed information about Mustache's tag types and advanced usage.

4. Let's modify the `ClientResource` class now by changing the `@Produces` annotation so that it uses the `View` class to generate HTML instead of plain text:

    ```
    @Produces(MediaType.TEXT_HTML)
    ```

5. Modify the `#showContact` method so that it returns a `ContactView` instance initialized with the contact representation fetched using the Jersey client. Import `com.dwbook.phonebook.views.ContactView` first:

    ```
    @GET
    @Path("showContact")
    public ContactView showContact
        (@QueryParam("id") int id) {
        WebResource contactResource = client.resource
            ("http://localhost:8080/contact/"+id);
        Contact c = contactResource.get(Contact.class);
        return new ContactView(c);
    }
    ```

How it works...

Let's test the UI. Rebuild the application, run it, and point your browser to `http://localhost:8080/client/showContact?id=2`. Instead of seeing the plain text response of the client, we now see an HTML table being rendered with the details of the contact with an ID equal to 2, as shown in the following screenshot:

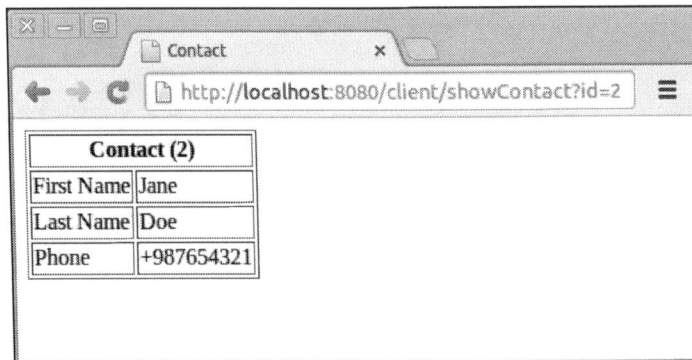

When we access the client's URL, it fetches the data by calling the appropriate service. The data is then passed as a `Contact` instance to the `ContactView` class that extends View, which uses the template engine to parse the designated template file, `contact.mustache`, and generate the HTML markup. The file extension indicates the template engine that shall be used.

There's more...

Mustache is not the only template engine supported by Dropwizard; there's also Freemarker. We chose Mustache over Freemarker to demonstrate Dropwizard's template capabilities since Mustache is a more logicless, agnostic programming language, and has implementations available for many programming languages.

On the other hand, Freemarker is Java-bound, has more programming capabilities, and can perform more complex tasks such as sanitizing the produced output.

If we were using Freemarker instead of Mustache for the previous example, the main table of the template would be the following:

```
<table border="1">
<tr>
  <th colspan="2">Contact (${contact.id})</th>
</tr>
<tr>
  <td>First Name</td>
  <td>${contact.firstName?html}</td>
</tr>
<tr>
  <td>Last Name</td>
  <td>{contact.lastName?html}</td>
</tr>
<tr>
  <td>Phone</td>
  <td>${contact.phone?html}</td>
</tr>
</table>
```

As you can see, the syntax of both template engines is similar. Note that while Mustache escapes variables by default, with Freemarker, you have to instruct the processor to sanitize the output by suffixing the variables with `?html`.

Serving static assets

There are cases where along with the HTML-based views, you need to serve static assets, such as CSS stylesheets, JavaScript files, or any other file that may be used by your application.

To do so, you may add an `AssetsBundle` instance on the `#bootstrap()` method, specifying the folder from where you can serve static files and also the URI that this folder will be mapped to. We will first need to import `io.dropwizard.assets.AssetsBundle` and modify the `pom.xml` file accordingly, declaring a dependency to the artifact dropwizard-assets..

For instance, if you want to serve a static stylesheet file named `stylesheet.css`, you'll have to store it under `src/main/java/resources/assets`.

```
b.addBundle(new AssetsBundle());
```

The `stylesheet.css` file would now be accessible from the `http://localhost:8080/assets/stylesheet.css` URL.

A

Testing a Dropwizard Application

Our application is ready. However, if we respect its stability, we have to make sure that we at least have its most important aspects covered by unit tests. You are probably familiar with unit testing and JUnit, but Dropwizard takes this a little bit further.

The `dropwizard-testing` module includes everything you need, such as JUnit and FEST assertions, in order to create tests for your application, right from small unit tests to bigger, full-fledged tests.

Creating a complete test for the application

Let's create a complete, fully automated integration test for our application. This test should start our application as we would normally do for a manual test, and perform some HTTP requests to the application's services which check how the application is responding.

Getting ready

When we first created our project using Maven in *Chapter 2, Creating a Dropwizard Application*, a JUnit dependency had been automatically added in our `pom.xml` file. We will replace it with Dropwizard's testing module, so let's remove it. Locate and delete the following dependency from the `pom.xml` file:

```
<dependency>
<groupId>junit</groupId>
<artifactId>junit</artifactId>
```

```
<version>3.8.1</version>
<scope>test</scope>
</dependency>
```

We will need the `dropwizard-testing` and `hamcrest-all` modules, so include them both in your `pom.xml` file:

```
<dependency>
    <groupId>io.dropwizard</groupId>
    <artifactId>dropwizard-testing</artifactId>
    <version>0.7.0-SNAPSHOT</version>
    </dependency>
    <dependency>
    <groupId>org.hamcrest</groupId>
    <artifactId>hamcrest-all</artifactId>
    <version>1.3</version>
</dependency>
```

How to do it...

Your project already has a test folder. During the generation of the default artifact, Maven created both `src/main/java` (where our application's source code lies) and `src/test/java` as a placeholder for our unit tests. Let's see what we need to place there in order to build our tests:

1. Create a new test class, `ApplicationTest`, within the `src/test/java/com/dwbook/phonebook` folder, extending the `ResourceTest` base class. This class needs to have two methods; `#setUp()`, in which we will prepare our mocked objects and add the required resources and providers to the memory inJersey server, and `#createAndRetrieveContact()`, where we will perform the actual test:

    ```
    package com.dwbook.phonebook;

    import static org.fest.assertions.
      api.Assertions.assertThat;

    import javax.ws.rs.core.MediaType;

    import org.junit.Before;
    import org.junit.ClassRule;
    import org.junit.Test;
    import com.dwbook.phonebook.representations.Contact;
    ```

```
import com.sun.jersey.api.client.Client;
import com.sun.jersey.api.client.ClientResponse;
import com.sun.jersey.api.client.WebResource;
import com.sun.jersey.api.client.filter.HTTPBasicAuthFilter;

import io.dropwizard.testing.junit.DropwizardAppRule;

public class ApplicationTest {

  private Client client;

  private Contact contactForTest = new Contact
    (0, "Jane", "Doe", "+987654321");

    @ClassRule
    public static final DropwizardAppRule
      <PhonebookConfiguration> RULE =
            new DropwizardAppRule<PhonebookConfiguration>
              (App.class, "config.yaml");

    @Before
    public void setUp() {
      client = new Client();
        // Set the credentials to be used by the client
        client.addFilter(new HTTPBasicAuthFilter
          ("wsuser", "wsp1"));
    }

    @Test
    public void createAndRetrieveContact() {
      // Create a new contact by performing the appropriate
        http request (POST)
        WebResource contactResource =
          client.resource("http://localhost:8080/contact");
    ClientResponse response = contactResource
      .type(MediaType.APPLICATION_JSON)
      .post(ClientResponse.class, contactForTest);
    // Check that the response has the appropriate
      response code (201)
```

```
assertThat(response.getStatus()).isEqualTo(201);

// Retrieve the newly created contact
String newContactURL =
  response.getHeaders().get("Location").get(0);
WebResource newContactResource =
  client.resource(newContactURL);
Contact contact =
  newContactResource.get(Contact.class);
// Check that it has the same properties
  as the initial one
assertThat(contact.getFirstName()).
  isEqualTo(contactForTest.getFirstName());
assertThat(contact.getLastName()).isEqualTo
  (contactForTest.getLastName());
assertThat(contact.getPhone()).isEqualTo
  (contactForTest.getPhone());
    }
  }
```

2. Our tests will run every time we issue the `mvn` package command, but they can also be executed on demand with the `test` command of `mvn`. For now, let's run the test on a clean application environment by issuing the following command:

   $ mvn clean test

   You will see that Maven will clean our target directory, start the application, and then run our tests successfully.

```
 ●  ⊖ ○   Terminal
    GET     /client/updateContact (com.dwbook.phonebook.resources.ClientResource)

INFO  [2014-01-04 15:56:18,619] org.eclipse.jetty.server.handler.ContextHandler: Started i.d.j.MutableServletContextHandler@1a501b5{/,null,AVAILABLE}
INFO  [2014-01-04 15:56:18,620] io.dropwizard.setup.AdminEnvironment: tasks =

    POST    /tasks/gc (io.dropwizard.servlets.tasks.GarbageCollectionTask)

INFO  [2014-01-04 15:56:18,626] org.eclipse.jetty.server.handler.ContextHandler: Started i.d.j.MutableServletContextHandler@1ce49a7{/,null,AVAILABLE}
INFO  [2014-01-04 15:56:18,634] org.eclipse.jetty.server.ServerConnector: Started application@111cedd{HTTP/1.1}{0.0.0.0:8080}
INFO  [2014-01-04 15:56:18,636] org.eclipse.jetty.server.ServerConnector: Started admin@242f84{HTTP/1.1}{0.0.0.0:8081}
Trying to authenticate user....
Tests run: 1, Failures: 0, Errors: 0, Skipped: 0, Time elapsed: 3.771 sec

Results :

Tests run: 1, Failures: 0, Errors: 0, Skipped: 0

[INFO] ------------------------------------------------------------
[INFO] BUILD SUCCESS
[INFO] ------------------------------------------------------------
[INFO] Total time: 7.879s
[INFO] Finished at: Sat Jan 04 17:56:19 EET 2014
[INFO] Final Memory: 17M/169M
[INFO] ------------------------------------------------------------
$
```

How it works...

Firstly, we defined our test data; that is, a `Contact` instance that we intend to create.

We initialized a `DropwizardAppRule<PhonebookConfiguration>` instance, which is described as a JUnit rule for starting and stopping your application at the start and end of a test class, allowing the test framework to start the application as you would normally do in order to perform a manual test. For this, we need to specify not only the main class of our application, but also the configuration file to be used.

Within the `#setUp()` method, we instantiated a REST client to help us with the HTTP requests to our application and also applied the necessary HTTP basic authentication filter since our web services require authentication.

The `#createAndRetrieveContact()` method wraps the actual test. Using the REST client, we are performing an HTTP POST request in order to create a new contact. After such a request, we expect an HTTP response with the `code 201 – Created` response. We test whether the response code is the one we expected with the `assertThat()` and `isEqual()` helper methods, which are provided by the **Fixtures for Easy Software Testing (FEST)** libraries. As stated on the home page of the FEST project (`http://code.google.com/p/fest/`):

> *"FEST is a collection of libraries, released under the Apache 2.0 license, whose mission is to simplify software testing. It is composed of various modules, which can be used with TestNG or JUnit."*

There's more...

We just showcased the use of the Dropwizard testing module in order to perform an integration test by booting an actual server that is connected to an actual database. This module is not limited to integration testing though. It is backed by JUnit, and you are able to use it for smaller (but critical) to larger unit tests and also for testing the correct serialization/deserialization of entities.

Adding health checks

A health check is a runtime test for our application. We are going to create a health check that tests the creation of new contacts using the Jersey client.

The health check results are accessible through the admin port of our application, which by default is 8081.

How to do it...

To add a health check perform the following steps:

1. Create a new package called com.dwbook.phonebook.health and a class named NewContactHealthCheck in it:

```
import javax.ws.rs.core.MediaType;
import com.codahale.metrics.health.HealthCheck;
import com.dwbook.phonebook.representations.Contact;
import com.sun.jersey.api.client.*;

public class NewContactHealthCheck extends HealthCheck {
    private final Client client;

    public NewContactHealthCheck(Client client) {
    super();
    this.client = client;
    }

    @Override
    protected Result check() throws Exception {
      WebResource contactResource = client
        .resource("http://localhost:8080/contact");
      ClientResponse response = contactResource.type(
        MediaType.APPLICATION_JSON).post(
          ClientResponse.class,
          new Contact(0, "Health Check First Name",
            "Health Check Last Name", "00000000"));
          if (response.getStatus() == 201) {
            return Result.healthy();
          } else {
            return Result.unhealthy("New Contact cannot
              be created!");
      }
    }
  }
}
```

2. Register the health check with the Dropwizard environment by using the HealthCheckRegistry#register() method within the #run() method of the App class. You will first need to import com.dwbook.phonebook.health. NewContactHealthCheck. The HealthCheckRegistry can be accessed using the Environment#healthChecks() method:

```
// Add health checks
e.healthChecks().register
("New Contact health check",
  new NewContactHealthCheck(client));
```

3. After building and starting your application, navigate with your browser to `http://localhost:8081/healthcheck`:

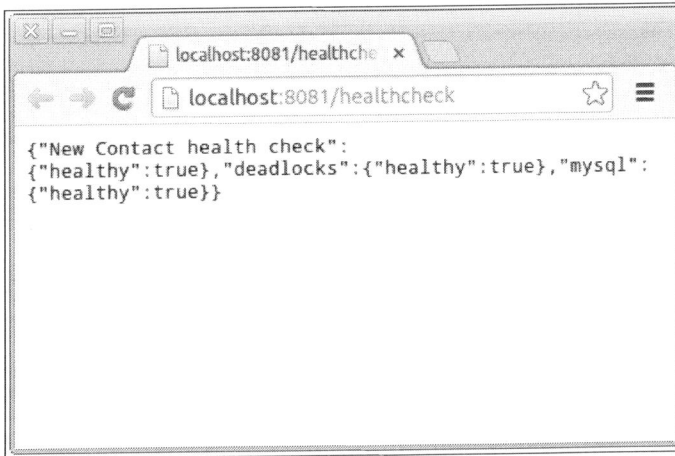

The results of the defined health checks are presented in the JSON format. In case the custom health check we just created or any other health check fails, it will be flagged as `"healthy":false`, letting you know that your application faces runtime problems.

How it works...

We used exactly the same code used by our `client` class in order to create a health check; that is, a runtime test that confirms that the new contacts can be created by performing HTTP POST requests to the appropriate endpoint of the `ContactResource` class. This health check gives us the required confidence that our web service is functional.

All we need for the creation of a health check is a class that extends `HealthCheck` and implements the `#check()` method. In the class's constructor, we call the parent class's constructor specifying the name of our check—the one that will be used to identify our health check.

In the `#check()` method, we literally implement a check. We check that everything is as it should be. If so, we return `Result.healthy()`, else we return `Result.unhealthy()`, indicating that something is going wrong.

Deploying a Dropwizard Application

Throughout this book, we have demonstrated and used the most important parts of a Dropwizard project. Our application is now ready, production ready. It is ready to be deployed on a server from where it can be accessed by everyone through the Internet.

Preparing the application for deployment

As you may have guessed, our application does not have many dependencies. Just check for your pom.xml file and look for the section where maven-compiler-plugin is declared.

```
<project xmlns="http://maven.apache.org/POM/4.0.0"
  xmlns:xsi="http://www.w3.org/2001/XMLSchema-instance"
  xsi:schemaLocation="http://maven.apache.org/POM/4.0.0
    http://maven.apache.org/maven-v4_0_0.xsd">
<modelVersion>4.0.0</modelVersion>
<groupId>com.dwbook.phonebook</groupId>
<artifactId>dwbook-phonebook</artifactId>
<packaging>jar</packaging>
<version>1.0-SNAPSHOT</version>
<name>dwbook-phonebook</name>
<url>http://maven.apache.org</url>
<!-- Maven Repositories -->
<repositories>
  <repository>
    <id>sonatype-nexus-snapshots</id>
    <name>Sonatype Nexus Snapshots</name>
```

```xml
      <url>http://oss.sonatype.org/content/repositories/snapshots</url>
        </repository>
    </repositories>
    <!-- Dependencies -->
    <dependencies>
      <dependency>
        <groupId>io.dropwizard</groupId>
        <artifactId>dropwizard-core</artifactId>
        <version>0.7.0-SNAPSHOT</version>
      </dependency>
      <dependency>
        <groupId>mysql</groupId>
        <artifactId>mysql-connector-java</artifactId>
        <version>5.1.6</version>
      </dependency>
      <dependency>
        <groupId>io.dropwizard</groupId>
        <artifactId>dropwizard-jdbi</artifactId>
        <version>0.7.0-SNAPSHOT</version>
      </dependency>
      <dependency>
        <groupId>io.dropwizard</groupId>
        <artifactId>dropwizard-client</artifactId>
        <version>0.7.0-SNAPSHOT</version>
      </dependency>
      <dependency>
        <groupId>io.dropwizard</groupId>
        <artifactId>dropwizard-auth</artifactId>
        <version>0.7.0-SNAPSHOT</version>
      </dependency>
      <dependency>
        <groupId>io.dropwizard</groupId>
        <artifactId>dropwizard-views-mustache</artifactId>
        <version>0.7.0-SNAPSHOT</version>
      </dependency>
      <dependency>
        <groupId>io.dropwizard</groupId>
        <artifactId>dropwizard-assets</artifactId>
        <version>0.7.0-SNAPSHOT</version>
      </dependency>
      <dependency>
        <groupId>io.dropwizard</groupId>
        <artifactId>dropwizard-testing</artifactId>
```

```xml
        <version>0.7.0-SNAPSHOT</version>
      </dependency>
      <dependency>
        <groupId>org.hamcrest</groupId>
        <artifactId>hamcrest-all</artifactId>
        <version>1.3</version>
      </dependency>
    </dependencies>
    <!-- Build Configuration -->
    <build>
      <plugins>
        <plugin>
          <groupId>org.apache.maven.plugins</groupId>
          <artifactId>maven-compiler-plugin</artifactId>
          <version>3.1</version>
          <configuration>
            <source>1.7</source>
            <target>1.7</target>
            <encoding>UTF-8</encoding>
          </configuration>
        </plugin>
        <plugin>
          <groupId>org.apache.maven.plugins</groupId>
          <artifactId>maven-shade-plugin</artifactId>
          <version>1.6</version>
          <configuration>
            <filters>
              <filter>
                <artifact>*:*</artifact>
                  <excludes>
                    <exclude>META-INF/*.SF</exclude>
                    <exclude>META-INF/*.DSA</exclude>
                    <exclude>META-INF/*.RSA</exclude>
                  </excludes>
              </filter>
            </filters>
          </configuration>
          <executions>
            <execution>
              <phase>package</phase>
                <goals>
                  <goal>shade</goal>
                </goals>
```

```
                <configuration>
                    <transformers>
                        <transformer
implementation="org.apache.maven.plugins.shade.resource.
ManifestResourceTransformer">
                            <mainClass>com.dwbook.phonebook.App</mainClass>
                        </transformer>
                    </transformers>
                </configuration>
            </execution>
        </executions>
    </plugin>
  </plugins>
 </build>
</project>
```

All that should be present on the server is the Java Runtime Environment of the version that is equal or greater to the one specified in the `<target>` element of the build plugin's configuration section.

How to do it...

Once we confirm that our dependencies (the Java versions) are satisfied, we can upload the JAR file through an FTP and run the application in the same way as we already do:

```
$ java -jar <applicationFilename.jar> server <configFileName.yaml>
```

How it works...

In our `pom.xml` file, we have all the required Maven parameters declared along with `maven-shade-plugin`, which allows us to build a single JAR file that includes all the third-party modules and libraries our application uses. Just remember to upload your config file on the server as well or create a new one with a possibly different setting, such as database connection details.

There's more...

There are many good reasons why you may wish to change the default port of your application from 8080 to something else.

This can be achieved with just a few additions to your configuration file: `config.yaml`. However, in order for these settings to work, we will need to add ServiceResourceTransformer in the build configuration by adding the following entry in the pom.xml file, within the `<transformers>` section: `<transformer implementation="org.apache.maven.plugins.shade.resource.ServicesResourceTransformer"/>`.

Add the section `server` and configure its properties as shown in the following code:

```
server:
    applicationConnectors:
        - type: http
          # The port the application will listen on
          port: 8181
    adminConnectors:
        - type: http
          # The admin port
          port: 8282
```

Multiple configuration files

A good practice is to maintain different sets of configuration files (YAML) for your application per environment. For instance, you will probably be using different databases for test and production environments, and it's better to keep the connection information in different files. In addition, you may want to have a more verbose log level on your development or test environment than in production. Depending on the nature and the complexity of your application, there would for sure be many additional reasons that you and your application would benefit by. Luckily, Dropwizard offers many settings that can be tweaked to match your application's needs.

Index

Thank you for buying
RESTful Web Services with Dropwizard

About Packt Publishing

Packt, pronounced 'packed', published its first book "*Mastering phpMyAdmin for Effective MySQL Management*" in April 2004 and subsequently continued to specialize in publishing highly focused books on specific technologies and solutions.

Our books and publications share the experiences of your fellow IT professionals in adapting and customizing today's systems, applications, and frameworks. Our solution based books give you the knowledge and power to customize the software and technologies you're using to get the job done. Packt books are more specific and less general than the IT books you have seen in the past. Our unique business model allows us to bring you more focused information, giving you more of what you need to know, and less of what you don't.

Packt is a modern, yet unique publishing company, which focuses on producing quality, cutting-edge books for communities of developers, administrators, and newbies alike. For more information, please visit our website: www.packtpub.com.

About Packt Open Source

In 2010, Packt launched two new brands, Packt Open Source and Packt Enterprise, in order to continue its focus on specialization. This book is part of the Packt Open Source brand, home to books published on software built around Open Source licences, and offering information to anybody from advanced developers to budding web designers. The Open Source brand also runs Packt's Open Source Royalty Scheme, by which Packt gives a royalty to each Open Source project about whose software a book is sold.

Writing for Packt

We welcome all inquiries from people who are interested in authoring. Book proposals should be sent to author@packtpub.com. If your book idea is still at an early stage and you would like to discuss it first before writing a formal book proposal, contact us; one of our commissioning editors will get in touch with you.

We're not just looking for published authors; if you have strong technical skills but no writing experience, our experienced editors can help you develop a writing career, or simply get some additional reward for your expertise.

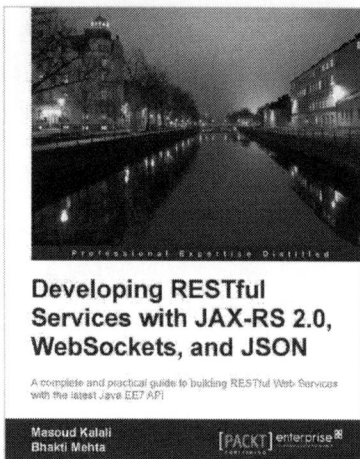

Developing RESTful Services with JAX-RS 2.0, WebSockets, and JSON

ISBN: 978-1-78217-812-5   Paperback: 128 pages

A complete and practical guide to building RESTful Web Services with the latest Java EE7 API

1. Learning about different client/server communication models including but not limited to client polling, Server-Sent Events, and WebSockets

2. Efficiently use WebSockets, Server-Sent Events, and JSON in Java EE applications

3. Learn about JAX-RS 2.0 new features and enhancements

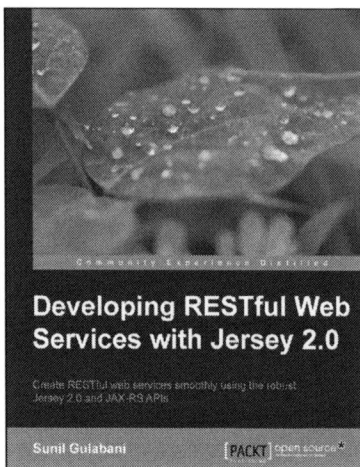

Developing RESTful Web Services with Jersey 2.0

ISBN: 978-1-78328-829-8   Paperback: 98 pages

Create RESTful web services smoothly using the robust Jersey 2.0 and JAX-RS APIs

1. Understand and implement the Jersey and JAX-RS APIs with ease

2. Construct top-notch server and client side web services

3. Learn about Server sent events, for showing real-time data

Please check **www.PacktPub.com** for information on our titles

ASP.NET Web API

ISBN: 978-1-84968-974-8   Paperback: 224 pages

Master ASP.NET Web API using .NET Framework 4.5 and Visual Studio 2013

1. Clear and concise guide to the ASP.NET Web API with plentiful code examples

2. Learn about the advanced concepts of the WCF-windows communication foundation

3. Explore ways to consume Web API services using ASP.NET, ASP.NET MVC, WPF, and Silverlight clients

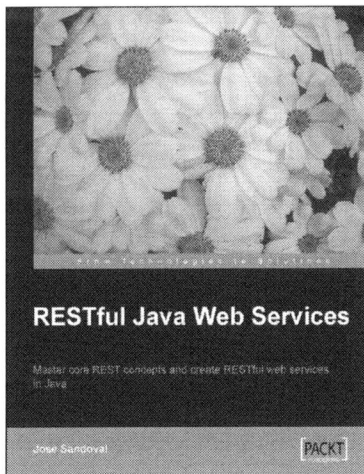

ASP.NET Web API

Build RESTful web applications and services on the .NET framework

Master ASP.NET Web API using .NET Framework 4.5 and Visual Studio 2013

Joydip Kanjilal   [PACKT] enterprise

RESTful Java Web Services

ISBN: 978-1-84719-646-0   Paperback: 256 pages

Master core REST concepts and create RESTful web services in Java

1. Build powerful and flexible RESTful web services in Java using the most popular Java RESTful frameworks to date (Restlet, JAX-RS based frameworks Jersey and RESTEasy, and Struts 2)

2. Master the concepts to help you design and implement RESTful web services

3. Plenty of screenshots and clear explanations to facilitate learning

RESTful Java Web Services

Master core REST concepts and create RESTful web services in Java

Jose Sandoval   PACKT

Please check **www.PacktPub.com** for information on our titles

23401437R00063

Printed in Great Britain
by Amazon